Dear Alison

Happy looking

lots of love
Bobby
xx

THE
LAD'S CHEF
COOKBOOK

THE LAD'S CHEF COOKBOOK

Bobby Jewell

INTRODUCTION

Guys, have you ever met a girl down the pub and told her you can cook? Or gone one step further, and offered to cook dinner for her and her mates after a day at the beach, only to realise you have nothing in the fridge or don't know what to cook? I know I have. Over the years, my mates and I have shared stories and given each other ideas and 'insider tips' on how to impress a girl through the wonders of cooking.

The Lad's Chef Cookbook will provide you with recipes to cook a kick-ass dinner. You will be treated to snacks, main courses and cocktails. To top it all off I am going to share with you some of my 'insider tips' to impress.

Hopefully, you will get that second date with that beautiful girl you met down the pub!

Enjoy and good luck!

Bobby

DEDICATION

For my wonderful family, thank you for standing by me.

Special thank you to Justine McKell for seeing potential in me and introducing me to my manager, Jason Williamson. You're a true star who has inspired me to give this a go. Jason, you took the punt and sent my photograph to the fabulous Linda Williams, who saw the same vision as you. Big Fella, thank you.

To Fiona, Linda, Diane, Lliane, Rochelle and all the team at New Holland, I am forever grateful for the confidence you have shown in me and for bringing The Lad's Chef Cookbook *to life!*

To my amazing personal assistant, Kirrily Bateup, who helped me with the finer details of this book.

And lastly to my right-hand man and head chef Wayne Kingsman, without your help I couldn't have completed this wonderful book, I thank you from the bottom of my heart.

ABOUT THE AUTHOR

Bobby Jewell grew up in Cambridge, England but now call Australia home. He is a qualified chef and loves to entertain. Bobby owns Sydney's only fancy dress restaurant—Tharen's Restaurant and Bar where there's a party every night of the week.

He loves windsurfing and enjoys a nice cold beer at the end of the day.

CONTENTS

A Young Guy's Kitchen Essentials — 12
Broke, Hungry & Missing Mum — 20
Sunday Barbecues — 38
Bring a Plate — 64
Dinner Parties — 78
Winter Warmers — 122
Romantic Dinners — 132
Friday Night with The Boys — 150
Hangover Cures — 160
Feeling Ill — 174
Party Time — 186

When I moved out of home, mum asked if I needed help setting up my first flat. Determined to do it myself, I said 'Nah mum, she'll be right!' Looking back, I had no idea what I needed in my kitchen to be able to cook—you forget you need utensils, bowls, chopping knives, and so on.

So guys, I've made it easier for you. Here's a list of what I recommend you have in your kitchen ... most of these items make great presents from your parents, grandparents, aunties and uncles. It might be uncool to ask, but it will save you a fortune!

A YOUNG GUY'S KITCHEN ESSENTIALS

Equipment

Knives—chef knife and a smaller knife (paring knife)

Knife sharpener—always have sharp knives in the kitchen

Selection of stainless steel mixing bowls of all sizes

Sieve and colander

Whisk

Chopping boards—I reckon you should always have a selection of them in different colours

Vegetable peeler

Wooden spoons

Two metal spoons

Pots and pans—get a large selection, get them on sale and never get pots with plastic handles

Multimixer/food processor—this will be the best thing you ever buy!

Good blender

Masher

Tongs

Dry Store/Cupboards

Bay leaves

Salt

Peppercorns

Soy sauce—light and dark

Worcestershire sauce

Balsamic vinegar

Curry powder

Cumin

Turmeric

Plain flour

Bicarbonate soda

Brown sugar

Palm sugar

Nutmeg

Sultanas

Jam

Icing sugar

Vanilla essence

Caster sugar

Pasta

Chocolate

Beer

White wine

Red wine

Olive/vegetable oil

Handy Terms

Baking is where food is cooked in an oven by dry heat.

Basting is when a small amount of fat is poured over the food while cooking to retain moisture and aid in colouring.

Boiling is the method of cookery where food is completely immersed in liquid and cooked at the boiling point of the liquid (for water it's 100°C/200°F/gas mark 1).

Blanching is when we par-cook foods in boiling water then immediately immerse in cold water or ice to stop the cooking process completely.

Braising is where we cook foods in a pot half-filled with liquid, covered tightly. The cooking liquids are often used for the sauce.

Deglazing is where you remove cooking sediment from the bottom of a roasting tray or pan with stock, wine or any liquid.

Pan frying is where food is cooked in a small amount of fat and turned with a palette knife or tongs.

Poaching is when we cook foods in liquid below boiling point. This is a very gentle form of cooking and is ideal for fish, eggs, red meat and chicken.

Roasting is where food is cooked in an oven and basted with fat.

Sautéing involves tossing food in a small amount of hot fat to colour and seal. Sauté comes from the French word 'to jump'.

Shallow frying is when food is cooked in a small amount of fat in a pan.

Simmering is a gentle form of boiling, on low heat.

Stewing is the slow cooking of food cut into pieces and cooked with minimum liquid. The food and liquid are served together.

Guys, it's OK to miss our mums. I have been missing my mum since moving to Australia. How great was it to have your ironing done, your bed made with fresh sheets, and of course a full fridge 24/7?

When I first left home, I always found myself broke and hungry. My fridge was always empty and I never had any cash. It's so bloody easy to just not eat! But these recipes are simple and will fill you up for ages. Anyone can fix these up!

The Pea & Ham Soup is one of the cheapest and easiest soups to make. I recommend making a big batch of the soup and freezing it. Remember that motto: cook once but feed for a week!

Chicken Kiev is my favourite. I think it was the first dish I ever cooked all by myself. It really is straightforward and tastes great with mash potato. Chicken Kiev makes me feel just like I am home with mum.

BROKE, HUNGRY & MISSING MUM

PEA & HAM SOUP

PREPARATION TIME: 15 minutes
COOKING TIME: 2 hours
SERVES: 2–4

INGREDIENTS:

25g (¾oz) butter
2 garlic cloves, crushed
1 red onion, chopped coarsely
1 carrot, chopped coarsely
800g (26oz) bacon, or hock bones
4 cups (1L/32fl oz) chicken stock
250g (6½oz) green peas, rinsed well
10g (1/3oz) parsley
pepper

METHOD:

In a saucepan on medium heat, melt the butter and add garlic, onion, carrot and bacon or bones. Cook for approximately 2 minutes to extract all the flavour.

Now add the stock and finally the peas. Bring this all to the boil and skim the top to remove the build up of impurities on the surface.

Cover and gently cook until peas are tender. This usually takes about 2 hours.

If you are using bacon bones, remove them from the soup now. Take the meat off the bones, discard the bones, shred the meat and return the meat to the pan.

Blend this all up using a blender, bar mix or your food processor.

Season with pepper only, the salt from the bacon should be enough.

This is an easy recipe that takes just under 15 minutes to prepare. If you're feeling a bit under the weather, you will feel better in no time after eating this. Remember: soups are a great way to get all the goodies back into your body. You can add pretty much anything to this recipe—by all means, experiment with flavours, but do your research first.

STUFFED SHOULDER OF LAMB

PREPARATION TIME: 30 minutes
COOKING TIME: 90 minutes
SATISFACTION VALUE: Nothing quite like mum's cooking!
SERVES: 2– 4

INGREDIENTS:

50g (1¾oz) chopped onion
1 garlic clove, crushed
1 sprig rosemary
1 teaspoon thyme
30g (1oz) roasted pine nuts
1 big handful baby spinach
20g (²/₃oz) butter
100g (3½oz) breadcrumbs
1 egg yolk
Roasting vegetables
(1 carrot, roughly chopped, 1 stick of celery roughly chopped, 4 garlic cloves roughly chopped)
1 shoulder of lamb
    (2–2.5kg/4–5lb—ask your butcher to debone it)
salt
pepper

METHOD:

Sautee onions, garlic, rosemary and thyme all together in a frying pan with butter. Mix your pine nuts and spinach in. Add your breadcrumbs and stir. To combine it all, put the egg yolk in. If the stuffing is a bit dry add a tiny bit of stock or water (not too much).

Preheat the oven to 200°C/400°F/gas mark 6. Lay your lamb shoulder on the chopping board then open it out. Put loads of salt and pepper in the middle and rub it in with your hands. Remember to be really generous at this stage—you don't want the meat to taste under-seasoned. Take your stuffing mix and place it on the open lamb shoulder. Roll firmly but not too tight as the stuffing will be squeezed out.

Now, you will need to tie it up with string so the stuffing doesn't fall out. Lightly season the outside of the lamb with salt, pepper and herbs.

Place the lamb in your vegetables in your roasting tray and cook in the oven, basting frequently. Turn oven down to 160°C/325°F/gas mark 2–3 after 20 minutes and cook for approximately another 30 minutes. Allow to rest for 15–20 minutes before carving.

Now for the sauce. Take your roasting tray and place it over the heat of the stove top. Heat it up until all the liquid starts bubbling, deglaze the pan with the red wine and add 100ml of stock and reduce. Serve with roast vegetables.

BAKED POTATOES WITH CHEESY BEANS

PREPARATION TIME: 10 minutes
COOKING TIME: 90 minutes
SATISFACTION VALUE: You'll fall asleep after it!
SERVES: 2

INGREDIENTS:

2 large potatoes (don't peel them as we need the skin to become crispy)
50g (1¾oz) butter
1 red onion, chopped finely
1 rasher bacon, chopped finely
½ medium carrot, chopped finely (because my Mum always said, 'Bobby, eat your carrots because it will help you see in the dark'!)
½ stalk celery, chopped finely
1 can (450g/14½oz) baked beans
60g (2oz) cheddar cheese. grated
salt
pepper

METHOD:

Preheat the oven to 180°C/350°F/gas mark 4. Chuck potatoes in a baking tray and cook them in the oven for 90 minutes.

Melt 10g (⅓oz) of butter in a saucepan on low heat. Now toss in the onion, bacon, carrot and celery and cook it til it sizzles! (the technical term for sizzling is 'sweating'!)

Adjust the heat to a low flame, making sure the onions and bacon aren't burning. Open your can of beans, chuck it in there and stir until the mixture boils. Turn the heat down and simmer for 15 minutes, stirring occasionally to avoid sticking.

Stir the cheese into the pan and mix well so all the ingredients are combined.

Take the potatoes out of the oven and chop them in half. Then cut your remaining butter up into 4 pieces and pop each piece inside a potato half. Cover the steaming potatoes in bean mix. Done!

This recipe is really easy, really cheap and doesn't take much preparation time at all. Cheesy Beans can also be cooked as a comfort dinner with a girlfriend—trust me, she will dig it in winter.

CHICKEN KIEV

PREPARATION TIME: 30 minutes
COOKING TIME: 20 minutes
SATISFACTION VALUE: Easier than it looks, tastier than it sounds
SERVES: 1

INGREDIENTS:

100g (3½oz) butter
1 tablespoon chopped parsley
1 garlic clove, crushed
1 chicken breast
20g (²/₃oz) flour
salt
pepper
1 egg, lightly beaten
¼ cup milk (optional)
100g (3½oz) breadcrumbs

METHOD:

Make flavoured butter by mixing 40g (1 ¹/₃oz) of the butter with parsley and garlic. Then mould it using cling-wrap into a cylinder shape.

Take your chicken breast and remove the fillet (the little flesh on the back of the chicken breast) carefully. Now take the chicken breast and make a small incision into the fattest part of the breast, carefully push your knife into the chicken to make a hole (big enough to push your butter into). Push the butter into this cavity and reshape the chicken breast so it is nice and plump.

It is time for crumbing your chicken breast. This stage is quite messy and by the end of the process, your hands will be covered with breadcrumbs. Place your flour onto a small plate and put a decent amount of salt and pepper into the flour mix (this is called seasoned flour).

Crack the egg into a glass or bowl, mixing it with a fork. Add a splash of milk if you want (this is called egg wash). Put the egg wash next to the flour. On a separate plate pour your breadcrumbs evenly across the plate.

Coat the chicken breast in the seasoned flour, dip it in the egg wash then coat the whole breast in the breadcrumbs (If you prefer a thicker coat, this step can be repeated).

Put the crumbed chicken breast on a new plate and pop it into the refrigerator for 30 minutes. Refrigerating the chicken breast will harden up the crumbing and help the breast to regain its shape.

Preheat oven to 180°C/350°F/gas mark 4. In a frypan, heat the remainder of the butter until it has melted. Take your Chicken Kiev from the fridge and place it into the butter. Cook until the chicken is a nice golden-brown colour. Then transfer the chicken to a baking tray and cook in the oven for approximately 15 minutes to finish cooking. Serve with Creamy Potato Swirls (see next page).

CREAMY POTATO SWIRLS

PREPARATION TIME: 30 minutes
COOKING TIME: 30 minutes
SATISFACTION VALUE: Warm and fuzzy
SERVES: 2

INGREDIENTS:

200g (6½oz) potatoes
20g (²/₃oz) butter
1 egg yolk
salt
pepper

METHOD:

Preheat the oven to 220°C/420°F/gas mark 7. Wash and peel potatoes, roughly cut and boil in enough water to just cover.

When cooked, drain well and push through a sieve, using a wooden spoon, into a clean bowl. Mix in the butter, salt and pepper and egg yolk.

Place lightly greased baking paper on a baking tray. Spoon or pipe your potato mix in four even scoops/swirls onto the tray. Brush with butter and cook in the oven until golden brown.

MUSHROOM RISOTTO

PREPARATION TIME: 10 minutes
COOKING TIME: 20 minutes
SATISFACTION VALUE: Guaranteed!
SERVES: 2

INGREDIENTS:

20g (²/₃oz) oyster mushrooms, chopped
30g (1oz) button mushrooms, chopped
50g (1²/₃ oz) butter
20g (²/₃oz) onion, chopped
100g (3½oz) arborio rice
50ml (1¾fl oz) white wine
300ml (8¼fl oz) chicken stock
25g (¾oz) parmesan cheese
30ml (1½fl oz) olive oil
30g (1oz) leek, sliced

METHOD:

First step, heat your mushrooms in butter until well browned then set aside. Sweat your onion in oil and add the rice. Mix well on a gentle heat. Add your white wine and some stock and bring it to the boil while stirring regularly. It is important that we keep stirring the risotto for 15 minutes through this process to get the best result.

Slowly keep adding your stock to the mixture until the rice is *al dente* (this means the rice is not too hard but not too soft). Add the parmesan and mix your pre-cooked mushrooms through. Voilà! The easiest and tastiest mushroom risotto ever! Brilliant!

My mum has always loved mushroom risotto. It is a great dish that will definitely sort you out if you are homesick. Mushroom Risotto can also be shared with your spunky flatmate or neighbour!

RHUBARB AND APPLE CRUMBLE

PREPARATION TIME: 45 minutes
COOKING TIME: 1 hour 15 minutes
SATISFACTION VALUE: Creamy, crunchy classic
SERVES: 4

INGREDIENTS:

20g (²/₃oz) butter
1 green apple, peeled, cored and diced into 1cm (¼inch) pieces
20g (²/₃oz) dark brown sugar
100g (3½oz) rhubarb, washed, trimmed and chopped into 5cm (2inch) pieces.
1 orange, zest and juice

CRUMBLE:

50g (1²/₃oz) dark brown sugar
1 teaspoon ground cinnamon
125g (4oz) plain flour
100g (3½oz) unsalted butter, chopped into small pieces
30ml (1½fl oz) cream
10g (¹/₃oz) brown sugar

METHOD:

Preheat the oven to 200°C/400°F/gas mark 6. Heat butter in a pan with apple and sugar. Cook until the apples are just starting to become tender. Add the rhubarb and continue cooking until the rhubarb is tender but not mushy. Add orange zest and juice to the rhubarb mix and spoon it into a baking dish or ramekin.

To make the crumble, mix dark brown sugar, cinnamon and flour in a bowl, and, using your fingertips, work your butter into the flour mix. Cover the fruit mix with the crumble and bake in oven until golden.

Whip the cream until glossy but not fully whipped. Spoon this out and serve it with the crumble, and sprinkle brown sugar over the top as garnish.

Barbecues are the easiest and best way to have mates around and to impress the ladies. Trust me, the opposite sex love a good barbecue just as much as your mates. Barbecues are a great way to showcase what a good host you are. You make a couple of salads, have some really nice fresh French bread, a good selection of meats and seafood and you're away.

Be careful that you don't make it just about beer and meat. You can do that when it is a 'mates only' barbecue.

Make sure you grab a couple of bottles of white wine and even one of sparkling wine. You will make a better impression if you have a couple of choices for people to chose from.

When the drinks are flowing, provide something delicious to munch on. A bowl of olives and a simple cheese platter with some quince paste and crackers are a good starting point.

You should treat the barbecue meat as the main course and have the olives and cheese, etc for entrée. This way your afternoon/evening has a nice structure to it, and food is always available. You don't want people getting too tipsy straight away.

SUNDAY BARBECUES

STEAK AND CHUNKY CHIPS

PREPARATION TIME: 15 minutes
COOKING TIME: 30 minutes
SATISFACTION VALUE: Steak … yum!
SERVES: 4

INGREDIENTS:

350g (11½oz) Pontiac potatoes
olive oil
4x 180g (6oz) steaks, either Scotch fillet or sirloin steaks
30g (1oz) butter, melted

METHOD:

Cut potatoes in half and chop into chip shapes. Place in pan and cover with water, boil until almost cooked. Preheat your oven to 200°C/400°F/gas mark 6 while your potatoes are boiling. Take a roasting tray, pour in some olive oil and place in the oven. Be careful because the oil will heat up and be very, very hot!

Strain your chips, rough them up in the strainer so they become a bit fluffy round the edges. Carefully take your oven tray with the hot oil out of the oven and place chips in the oil. Try to coat every chip. Cook in the oven for 20 minutes.

Take your mates and your steaks over to the barbecue and grab yourself a beer on the way. Make sure you've seasoned your steaks with salt and pepper as you like them. Brush the steaks with the melted butter. Ensure the barbecue is piping hot, have a big sip of beer and pop your steaks on the barbecue.

Go talk to your mates and when you've drunk half your beer (or approximately 5 minutes later) turn your steaks over. When you've got one more sip left of your beer (approximately another 3 minutes) take the steaks off and rest them for 5 minutes. This will allow the meat to relax and become tender.

Remove chips from the oven. They should be golden brown and crunchy. Place them in a bowl lined with paper towels to remove any excess oil, season with loads of salt and serve with your steaks and some mustard or tomato ketchup.

WITLOF AND ROCKET SALAD

PREPARATION TIME: 5 minutes
COOKING TIME: 5 minutes
SATISFACTION VALUE: Light and tasty
SERVES: 2

INGREDIENTS:

2 witlofs
a big handful of rocket
1 beurre bosc pear, cored, sliced finely
200g (6½oz) haloumi
1 tablespoon olive oil
½ a lemon

METHOD:

Cut the stems off the witlof, and separate each leaf. Place into a bowl and add rocket. Finely slice pear and add to the salad mix.

Slice haloumi into 6 portions of 1cm (¼ inch) thickness and place into a hot, non-stick frying pan. Cook for 20 seconds on either side and immediately remove from pan and place onto paper towels to drain excess fat. Set aside.

Put your olive oil in a small bowl. Squeeze as much juice from the half lemon as you can and whisk ferociously with a fork until it becomes thick and creamy. Add a pinch of salt and pepper to season the dressing.

Add haloumi to salad mix, drizzle the dressing over the top and toss very gently before serving.

This dish can be used to spunk up a steak or be served on its own for that cute vegetarian lady you fancy.

COLA-MARINATED LAMB CHOPS

PREPARATION TIME: 5 minutes
COOKING TIME: 30 minutes
SATISFACTION VALUE: Amazing
SERVES: 4

INGREDIENTS:

1kg (2lb) lamb chops
salt
pepper
1 x 375ml (12fl oz) can of cola
100ml (3½fl oz) red wine
1 sprig rosemary
15ml (½fl oz) olive oil

METHOD:

Season your lamb chops with salt and pepper. In a bowl, combine the cola, red wine, rosemary and a tiny bit of olive oil. Put the lamb chops in a bowl with the marinade, then cover with cling wrap and refrigerate for 30 minutes.

Cook on a hot barbecue for approximately 1 minute each side of the lamb chop and serve with witlof salad. Don't forget to rest the chops for a few minutes before serving!

Seriously—if you marinate some meat in cola it makes even the worst cut of meat that anyone has brought around for you taste tender and delicious. Must be something they put in it!

MARINATED BARBECUE SALMON

PREPARATION TIME: 10 minutes
COOKING TIME: 10 minutes
MARINADE TIME: 60 minutes or more.
SERVES: 4

INGREDIENTS:

4 x 180g (4½oz) salmon fillets
200ml (6½fl oz) orange juice
200ml (6½fl oz) soy sauce
2 garlic cloves crushed
3 tablespoons tomato sauce
3 tablespoons peanut butter
1 tablespoon honey
10g (1/3oz) crushed fresh ginger

METHOD:

Combine salmon in a bowl with all ingredients. Refrigerate for at least one hour.

Grill the fish on the barbecue, flesh-side down, while basting the fillets with the leftover marinade. It should be cooked in about 7 minutes.

BARBECUE GARLIC AND CHILLI PRAWNS

PREPARATION TIME: 10 minutes
COOKING TIME: 10 minutes
MARINADE TIME: 60 minutes
SERVES: 4 or more

INGREDIENTS:

200ml (6½fl oz) olive oil
3 fresh chillies
3 garlic cloves, crushed
10g (1/3oz) fresh ginger, chopped or crushed
1 lemon, whole
1kg (2lb) uncooked prawns (either whole or peeled)

METHOD:

Combine the olive oil, chilli, garlic and ginger (chopped or crushed) into a bowl. Zest your lemon into this bowl as well.

Now add the juice of that lemon and whisk everything up until it is all combined.

Put the prawns in the marinade and refrigerate for 60 minutes.

Cook on the barbecue until done. This should take a maximum 10 minutes. If you are cooking them whole (with shells), make sure you really crisp them up so the shells are crunchy not chewy.

Don't forget to put out a clean bowl for the prawn shells, and a bowl with fresh water and lemon juice as a finger bowl. Having a hand towel handy would be good too!

This is a great way to cook prawns. If you barbecue them well enough, you will be able to eat the whole prawn, legs and all! Warning—some of your guests may think you are mad or feel threatened by the little sea creature, so peel their prawns before cooking if they prefer.

JUG OF SUMMER PIMM'S

PREPARATION TIME: 10 minutes
COOKING TIME: Zilch
SATISFACTION VALUE: Refreshing!
SERVES: 4

INGREDIENTS:

ice
90ml (3¼fl oz) Pimm's
60ml (2fl oz) gin
15ml (²/₃fl oz) vermouth
1L (32fl oz) dry ginger ale
handful of strawberries, hulled and chopped
½ a cucumber, peeled and chopped
1 lemon, sliced
2 sprigs of mint

METHOD:

Put your ice in the jug followed by Pimm's, gin, vermouth (extra dry) and fill to the top with dry ginger ale. Throw strawberries, lemon, mint and cucumber into jug. Stir and serve.

Guys, seriously! Pimm's is not a crap drink! It's wicked! If you smash this jug out at a gathering, everyone will love it. I reckon most of the ladies will think you are pretty classy. It's a dead set winner!

BARBECUE PORK CHOPS

PREPARATION TIME: 10 minutes
COOKING TIME: 15 minutes
MARINADE TIME: 2 hours or overnight
SATISFACTION VALUE: Chop Chop!
SERVES: 4

INGREDIENTS:

6 fresh basil leaves, roughly chopped
2 sprigs of rosemary
80ml (2¾fl oz) olive oil
125ml (4fl oz) fresh lemon juice
1 teaspoon lemon zest
2 garlic cloves, crushed
4 pork chops

METHOD:

Roughly chop the basil leaves and remove the rosemary from the stalks.

Combine oil, lemon juice, zest, herbs and garlic in a bowl to form a nice marinade. Refrigerate the pork chops for a minimum of 2 hours. I like to do this the night before so the flavours can really mix through.

Cook on a hot barbecue for about 12 minutes, turning after 6 minutes, until the liquid from the pork runs clear. Brush the chops with the marinade.

SAUSAGE SIZZLE WITH BEER, ONIONS AND TOMATO RELISH

PREPARATION TIME: 10 minutes
COOKING TIME: 15 minutes
SATISFACTION VALUE: Everyone loves snags
SERVES: 8–10

INGREDIENTS:

½ red onion, diced finely
2 tomatoes, diced
50ml (1⅔fl oz) tomato sauce
50ml (1⅔fl oz) barbecue sauce
salt
pepper
1kg (2lb) sausages (beef, pork or lamb—your choice!)
1 white onion, sliced
250ml (8fl oz) beer (whatever you're drinking)
10ml (½fl oz) white vinegar
½ teaspoon caster sugar
2 French breadsticks
dash of tabasco sauce

METHOD:

To make the tomato relish, place the red onion into a pan. Cook with a tiny bit of oil until soft. Add the chopped-up tomato, tomato sauce, barbecue sauce, some salt and pepper, white vinegar and sugar. Cook until the mixture reduces.

On a hot barbecue, cook your sausages until nicely brown on the outside but not overcooked.

Meanwhile, cook white onion on the barbecue until they just turn brown, then pour beer over the top of the mixture.

Cut French stick up into sandwich-size portions, cut through the middle of each portion, making sure to not go all the way through.

Stick your sausage in the French stick, top with onions and serve with tomato relish.

TRADITIONAL TIRAMISU

PREPARATION TIME: 15 minutes
COOKING TIME: 30 minutes
SATISFACTION VALUE: Mouth-watering
SERVES: 4

INGREDIENTS:

2 eggs, separated ('coz they argue all the time!)
65g (2¼oz) caster sugar
200g (6½oz) mascarpone
15ml (²/₃fl oz) rum
10ml (²/₃fl oz) Kahlua or Frangelico
110ml (3¾fl oz) espresso coffee
1 packet of Savoiardi biscuits (sold at all major supermarkets)
10g (¹/₃oz) cocoa powder
50g (1²/₃oz) grated cooking chocolate

METHOD:

Whisk your egg yolks and sugar together until pale. In a separate bowl, beat the egg whites to form nice fluffy peaks.

Lightly mix the yolk mixture with the mascarpone cream. Then gradually fold in the egg whites.

Mix your rum, liqueur and coffee together in a bowl and dip your biscuits into the mixture (quickly, so they don't become soggy).

Arrange biscuits in a layer on the bottom of your glass or a small rectangular cake tin. Spread on a layer of mascarpone mixture, repeating layers until all your ingredients have been used up.

Sprinkle the top with cocoa powder and chocolate shavings. Refrigerate for 2–3 hours before serving.

What barbecue would be complete without a Tiramisu? Have this prepped in your refrigerator, so after the barbecue or whenever you rock on home you can dig in and satisfy those post-drink munchies!

Being invited over to someone's house is a treat, but you have to turn up with something. Usually a bottle of wine and a dish of some sort. Trust me you can just bring wine, but if you turn up as a young lad with a dish—my god you will have them eating out of your hands all night long!

Remember, dress smart and remember your manners. Please and thank you go a long way.

BRING A PLATE

BABAGANOUJ DIP

PREPARATION TIME: 10 minutes
COOKING TIME: 20 minutes
SATISFACTION VALUE: Looking good
SERVES: 4

INGREDIENTS:

1 medium eggplant
1 garlic clove
½ teaspoon ground cumin seeds
50g (1$^2/_3$oz) tahina paste
juice of half a lemon
30ml (1$^1/_3$fl oz) olive oil

METHOD:

Preheat oven to 200°C/400°F/gas mark 6. Roast the whole eggplant in the oven for 15 minutes.

Leave eggplant to cool, then peel and puree with garlic, cumin, tahina paste, lemon juice and olive oil. Season to taste.

This is great for a party served with celery sticks, carrot sticks, crackers, etc.

BRESAOLA AND TOMATO SALAD WITH BOCCONCINI

PREPARATION TIME: 15 minutes
COOKING TIME: 10 minutes
SATISFACTION VALUE: Full of culture!
SERVES: 2–4

INGREDIENTS:

8 tomatoes, sliced
250g (8oz) bocconcini
bunch of basil
40 slices Bresaola
100ml (3½fl oz) extra virgin olive oil
50ml (1¾fl oz) good-quality balsamic vinegar
salt
pepper

METHOD:

Slice tomatoes and lay out on a flat salad dish. Rip bocconcini apart roughly and spread it all over the tomatoes. Sprinkle a few basil leaves on top of the bocconcini and tomatoes and lay the bresaola over the top of that.

Season with salt and pepper, then drizzle with balsamic and extra virgin olive oil.

If you are freaking out because you don't know what Bresaola is, don't! It's a type of dried, salted beef and can be replaced with Parma ham, some great shaved prosciutto, or left out all together.

CHEESE PLATTER

PREPARATION TIME: 30 minutes
SATISFACTION VALUE: You will feel like a pro!
SERVES: 6–10 people

INGREDIENTS:

One small wheel of Brie or Camembert (about 200g/6½oz)
A wedge of blue cheese (about 100g/3½oz)
A wedge of nice cheddar (100g/3½oz)
If you can find a smoked cheese in the supermarket (about 150g/5oz), then grab that as well
Some paté would be nice—cracked black pepper is my favourite
grapes
Some quince paste
And for goodness sake—remember the CRACKERS!

METHOD:

Don't just put it all on one platter. Pull out the nice serving platter your aunt gave you for Christmas, and cut the cheeses into triangles (decent sized ones of course). Evenly place them on the platter. Be creative with your triangle patterns; don't let the cheeses look cluttered. If you need to, get out the second platter your other aunt gave you for Christmas.

Remember to put the cheese knife on there for cutting and spreading the condiments onto the crackers.

If you feel you know nothing about cheese don't worry, because most of us don't either!

QUICHE LORRAINE

PREPARATION TIME: 10 minutes
COOKING TIME: 20 minutes
SERVES: 2–4

INGREDIENTS:

Short crust pastry base/quiche shell
50g (1^2/$_3$oz) ham
40g (1^1/$_3$oz) grated cheese
1 egg
60ml (2fl oz) milk
60ml (2fl oz) cream
10g (1/$_3$oz) chives

METHOD:

Preheat the oven to 180°C/350°F/gas mark 4. Line a quiche mould with short crust pastry (or buy a pre-made pastry shell). Prick holes in the top of the pastry with a fork. Cover it with baking paper and place some uncooked rice on top of the baking paper to weigh it down on to the pastry so that when it bakes, it does not rise. This may sound complicated, but it is easy. It's called 'blind baking'. Bake it in the oven for 10–15 minutes. Remove the baking paper and the rice. You might want to keep the rice and re-use it the next time you 'blind bake'.

After pastry has cooled, sprinkle ham and cheese over it. Mix egg, milk and cream and whisk it all together. Season it and strain it through a sieve into the pastry shell on top of the ham and cheese. Sprinkle some chopped chives over the top. Bake for 15 minutes or until nicely browned on top.

One of the classics and by far the easiest ever … you can take this anywhere and people will love it!

SAUSAGE ROLLS

PREPARATION TIME: 10 minutes
COOKING TIME: 20 minutes
SATISFACTION VALUE: Homemade Sausage rolls! Champ!
SERVES: 2–4

INGREDIENTS:

2 sheets of puff pastry
60g (2oz) onion, finely diced
200g (6½oz) sausage mince
10g (1/3oz) chopped parsley
salt
pepper
1 egg, lightly beaten

METHOD:

Cut your puff pastry into 10cm (4inch) wide strips. Sweat your onion, then, in a mixing bowl, combine onion with sausage mince and parsley. Using your fingers, mix it well. Shape mixture into a 2cm (¾ inch) roll.

Preheat oven to 220°C/420°F/gas mark 7. Place meat on pastry. Moisten edges of pastry, fold over and seal. Cut into approximately 8cm (3 inch) lengths, brush with beaten egg and score top with a knife. Transfer to a baking tray and cook in oven for approximately 20 minutes.

Now, dinner parties can be a bit daunting, but don't worry. If you're hosting one, then you must be really wanting to show off to a girl. By this stage you should have had her over for a barbecue and at least one comfort dinner at home in front of the TV.

Remember things for a dinner party:

- Table needs to be well presented—napkins and nicely polished cutlery.
- Candles make for a brilliant atmosphere—get tea lights and pop them in glasses
- Three courses evenly spread—don't rush, but you have to feed your guests.

Have a good sparkling wine for starting, then a good-value white and a great red. Ask the dude in the bottl-o to advise you if you are not sure—that's what they are there for.

DINNER PARTIES

TEN FASHION TIPS

- Know your neck size. You should be able to fit one finger between your collar and your neck when your shirt is fully buttoned.

- A tie's stripes should always be bolder than a shirt's.

- It is OK not to wear socks in summer, but only if you give your sweaty shoes a break every other day.

- An invitation saying 'black-tie optional' implies you can choose between black-tie and a suit, but it really means black-tie.

- Know the nuances of khaki pants? Don't roll up the cuffs to your calves like your searching for pippies, unless you actually are collecting pippies.

- Never put eyewear, your phone, an ink pen or a bulging key ring in your trouser pockets.

- A wallet is for credit cards only, cash goes in a money clip in your front pocket.

- Your sunnies should contrast with, not mimic, the shape of your face.

- It is acceptable to wear your jeans five to ten times between washings, but fewer if they get visibly dirty or baggy at the knee.

- The five terms your hairdresser will understand are thinned out, layered, choppy, razored and textured.

STEAK TARTAR

PREPARATION TIME: 15 minutes
COOKING TIME: 15 minutes
SATISFACTION VALUE: Totally superior
SERVES: 2

INGREDIENTS:

100g (3½oz) fresh beef fillet tail
30g (1oz) onions, diced
30g (1oz) gherkins, finely diced
10g (⅓oz) anchovies, chopped
20g (⅔oz) capers, drained, chopped
Worcestershire sauce
1 egg yolk
1 teaspoon Tabasco sauce
2 slices bread (for melba toast)
1 garlic clove

METHOD:

Finely chop the beef tail. Mix onion, gherkins, capers, anchovies, Worcestershire sauce, some salt and pepper and have a quick taste. Add a couple of drops of Tabasco.

Place the meat in a circular mound onto a plate. Crack an egg and put your yolk dead centre in the middle. For the melba toast chop the crusts off the bread, cut the bread diagonally into two triangles, drizzle with olive oil, rub it with your garlic clove, sprinkle with salt, and pepper on the top of it and pop it in the oven for about 3 minutes.

Don't let this scare you; people have been eating raw meat since the dinosaurs roamed. There's nothing better for your body than this! Pure protein, great for the gym, so healthy and above all, people will think you are a legend in the kitchen if you serve this! Beef fillet tail is the end part of the eye fillet centre cut.

PAN FRIED KINGFISH WITH BLANCHED GREENS

PREPARATION TIME: 10 minutes
COOKING TIME: 15 minutes
SATISFACTION VALUE: Fit and healthy
SERVES: 2

INGREDIENTS:

150g (5oz) of green beans,
150g (5oz) butter
1 lemon, halved
100ml (3½fl oz) white wine
2 x 150g (5oz) fillets of kingfish (ask your fish shop to cut and de-bone them for you)
50ml (1¾fl oz) vegetable oil
8 spears of asparagus (spears are sticks)
10ml (½fl oz) olive oil

METHOD:

Wash your veg and chop the top and tail off the beans, removing the stringy part.

Cut the butter into small cubes. Squeeze the lemon juice out of the lemon into a pan and pour the wine in the pan too. Place pan on the stove (don't turn the stove on just yet) and leave for later.

Heat a pot of salted water on the stove—this is for blanching your veg. Preheat your oven to 180°C/350°F/gas mark 4.

Heat a frying pan on the stove. Wait until the pan starts to smoke, then take it off the heat, add the vegetable oil and put it back on the heat, but turn the heat down to medium.

Put the fish in the pan, skin side first. Use tongs to make sure the skin doesn't stick to the pan. Now season the flesh of your fish with lots of salt and pepper while it is cooking in the pan. When the fish is easily moving around the pan you can tip some of the oil out, but careful—it's HOT!

Turn the fish over and continue cooking it for another 5 minutes before turning the heat off. Leaving the fish in the pan, transfer the pan to the oven for 10 minutes until cooked through.

While the fish is in the oven, put the beans and asparagus in the boiling water and finish the sauce by heating the wine and lemon juice mixture until it boils. Whisk in the butter slowly—this should take approximately 3 minutes. The sauce will begin to thicken. Season with salt and pepper.

Remove the vegetables from the water and lay them on the base of your serving plates. Take the fish out of the oven using oven mitts. (Remember, it's HOT.) Pop the fish on top of the greens.

Pour the sauce over the side of the dish or fish as you please. Drizzle with olive oil and Bingo! Done.

GRANDMA'S SEMOLINA WITH BLUEBERRY JAM

PREPARATION TIME: 5 minutes
COOKING TIME: 10 minutes
SATISFACTION VALUE: Keeping Grandmas happy
SERVES: 2

INGREDIENTS:

2 tablespoons semolina
1 tablespoon of caster sugar
1 pint (500ml/16fl oz) milk
1 teaspoon Bramble (blackcurrant) Jelly

METHOD:

Mix all ingredients together in a pot and stir. Bring to the boil on a medium heat and keep stirring for 3–4 minutes. It will start to thicken and might look weird, but it's so great.

Serve with a teaspoon of jelly in the middle.

Now, my Grandma has been serving this as a dessert for many years and I was hooked on it as a young kid. It is really easy and quick to prepare. It makes for a never-before-seen winner to round the night off. Boom! Nailed it!

THE SUNDAY ROAST

Roast dinners are so easy and a great way to round off the week. Most of them can be prepped before you hit the beach or go to the football, or even before you get a few sneaky drinks in down the pub. If you have a roast ready to go, you can either leave it in the oven while you're out (provided someone else is home, of course!) or you can chuck it in when you get home and dinner will be on the table an hour later. Timers on ovens are a blessing as well, but we'll leave that for another day.

NOW THIS IS SERIOUS GUYS SO READ CAREFULLY.

When handling raw chicken it's important to be aware that chicken is a high risk food. The majority contain food poisoning bacteria. If it is handled incorrectly or left out in the danger zone (4°C–6°C/39°–45°F) for too long, the bacteria will rapidly grow to dangerous levels.

Defrosting is also important, as, if defrosted out of the refrigerator, bacteria will also increase rapidly. When you move from chicken to other foods you must always clean all your equipment thoroughly to prevent cross contamination. Chicken must be cooked all the way through so that all the bacteria are destroyed.

Don't defrost chicken in hot water! It damages the cell structure and the excess loss of juices will result in your chicken being dry once it's cooked! Now that's that!

CUTS OF CHICKEN

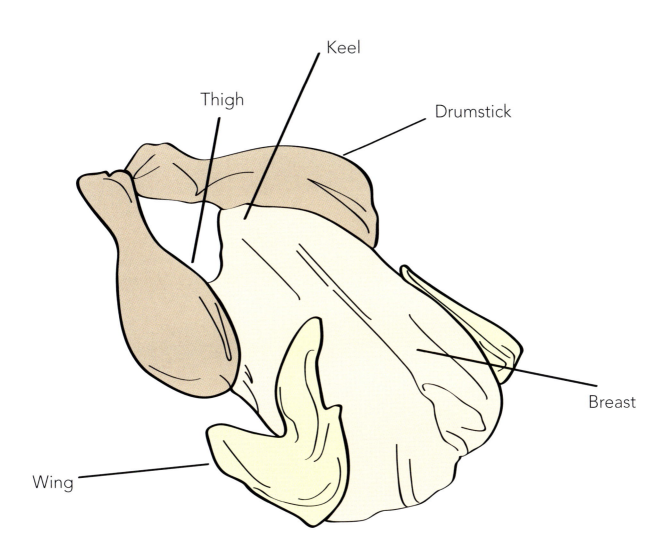

WHOLE ROAST CHICKEN WITH LEMON AND THYME

PREPARATION TIME: 20 minutes
COOKING TIME: 1.5 hours
SERVES: 4

INGREDIENTS:

1 whole chicken
25g ($^2/_3$oz) butter
1 lemon
1 teaspoon thyme
1 carrot, chopped roughly
1 onion, chopped roughly
3 cloves of garlic
10g ($^1/_3$oz) flour
250ml (8fl oz) white wine (or water, if you prefer)

METHOD:

Preheat oven to 180°C/350°F/gas mark 4. Give the chicken a wash then place it on your bench.

Rub the butter under the skin of the chicken being very careful not to break or rip the skin. Rub the butter along the top, massage into the legs and over the rest of the chicken.

Chop the lemon in half, slice off one slice and place underneath the skin. Shove one clove of garlic and the remaining lemon into the chicken's cavity, along with the thyme. Place carrot and onion on the bottom of your roasting tray.

Season the chicken with salt and pepper. Sit the chicken on top of the onions and carrots; add remaining garlic cloves.

Chuck your chook in the oven for 1 hour and 20 minutes. The butter will make the chicken golden and the skin will be crispy. To check if the chicken is done, pull the leg off and stick in a knife. If the juices run clear, then your chicken is cooked. If you see a little bit of blood, leave it in for another 20 minutes. The lemon and the butter will keep the chicken nicely basted and moist.

Once your chicken is cooked, rest it on a chopping board and cover in foil to keep it warm.

FOR YOUR GRAVY:

Take your roasting tray, place it on top of the stove and turn on the heat. Add flour and mix all the goodness and the roasted garlic into the pan. Then deglaze the pan by pouring in the white wine (or water) and stir for about 5 minutes until the mixture reduces. Season to taste. This is wicked gravy!

PORK SHOULDER WITH BAKED APPLES AND POTATOES

PREPARATION TIME: 10 minutes
COOKING TIME: 6 hours—definitely jump in the pool or watch a movie while this baby is cooking
SERVES: 6

You have to eat this dish with the apples—the pork just melts in your mouth with the sweetness of the apples—mmmmm

INGREDIENTS:

1 pork shoulder (350g/11½oz)
2 onions, chopped into quarters
8 garlic cloves
4 apples (2 roughly chopped and 2 halved)
2 stalks celery
2 carrots, peeled and halved lengthways
6 bay leaves
200ml (6fl oz) white wine
600ml (19½fl oz) stock
10g (1/3oz) brown sugar
10g (1/3oz) sultanas
salt
sugar (optional)
pepper

METHOD:

Preheat your oven to 220°C/420°F/gas mark 7. Put the pork shoulder on a chopping board with the skin-side up and cut the skin. They should be about one centimetre apart. Don't cut too deep as you just want to score the skin to make crackling. Do not cut into the meat. (I recommend getting your butcher to do this for you.)

Rub loads of salt all over the skin and into the scores you have made. Add a little sugar to the salt, this will complement the apples later.

Turn the shoulder over and season the inside with salt and pepper, remember it's a big piece of meat so don't be shy with the seasoning!

Now place your pork into a roasting tray and put it into the hot oven for 30 mins. This starts the cooking and helps create a wicked crackling.

After 30 mins you will see that the crackling has started to lift up and begin hardening. Turn the heat down to 170°C/335°F/gas mark 2–3.

You can at this stage cover the shoulder with foil, it may stop the crackling from burning. I usually don't bother! Leave in the oven for another 4 hours—go have a swim or get some drinks with the boys and invite some girls over for dinner. Don't get legless—you have to finish this dish!

Remove the pork from the oven and cover with the fat that's built up in the bottom of the tray, using a spoon to do this. This adds some more moisture to the pork.

Carefully lift the pork out of the tray and onto your chopping board. Place the chopped onions, garlic, chopped apples, celery, carrots and bay leaves into the tray. If there is a lot of fat in the tray you can remove some, but I think it all adds to the flavour.

Place the pork back on top of the vegies and roast in the oven for another hour. Add the halved apples to the outside of the shoulder in either corner of the roasting tray. Put a knob of butter on each and sprinkle with brown sugar and sultanas.

Now the pork should be so soft and ripping away easily. Carefully move the pork to your serving plate, spooning away any excess fat from the roasting tray. Then put the roasting tray on the stove over medium heat and add your white wine and let this bubble away.

Add the stock and garlic and mash the veg around. Pass the sauce through a sieve pushing hard to mush it all through. Serve with baked apples and roast veg.

BAKED APPLES

PREPARATION TIME: 15 minutes
COOKING TIME: 10 minutes
SERVES: 1–2

INGREDIENTS:

1 apple, peeled and cored
10g (1/3oz) castor Sugar
10g (1/3oz) butter, melted
10g (1/3oz) sultanas

METHOD:

Preheat the oven to 180°C/350°F/gas mark 4. Cut apple into slices and place in an ovenproof dish. Sprinkle with caster sugar and sultanas.

Pour butter on top and cook in oven until mixture golden brown. This takes about 10 minutes. Serve with the cooking liquid as a sauce.

I love pork—when this dish is cooked it's so soft and tender that you can pull the pork apart into strings. It's a definite crowd-pleaser and everyone you invite home will love it.

SWEET AND EASY ROASTED VEGETABLES

PREPARATION TIME: 10 minutes
COOKING TIME: 20 – 30 minutes
SERVES: As many or as little as you like! Depends on how many you succeeded in inviting to dinner!

INGREDIENTS:

Potatoes
Carrots
Onions
Pumpkin
Sweet potato
Zucchini
Parsnips
olive oil
2 cloves chopped garlic
1 sprig rosemary
20ml (1/3oz) sunflower oil (or vegetable oil)

METHOD:

For potatoes, it's always good to boil them before baking then strain them. In the strainer, you can fluff them up so that the fluffy bits will go nice and crispy when cooked in the oven. The potatoes will take longer than all the other vegetables.

Place some oil in an oven tray and put into the oven to heat up. Once the oil is heated, chuck your fluffy potatoes into the hot oil and return to the oven. While they cook you can prepare your other vegetables.

Chop up the carrots, onions, pumpkin, sweet potato, zucchini and parsnips into similar size pieces. Mix them in a bowl with some olive oil, garlic and rosemary. After potatoes have cooked for 15 minutes add other vegetables on to the tray. Remember to shake the pan occasionally so your veg doesn't stick and keep an eye on them so they don't burn. They should take about 45 minutes to cook.

A CRAZY 'GAME'

It's easy to impress people by using different meats and birds to cook with. Don't be scared of game meat, it usually tastes nicer and girls will think you are a culinary king when you start chatting in a bar and telling them that you can cook 'slow-cooked duck and marinated pheasant'. Putty in your hands…

Game used to be used only in the catering industry because it relied on the hunting seasons for different animals. Today, we have the pleasure and convenience of heading down to our local butchers for some hunting of our own—we can grab some duck, guinea fowl, pheasant or spatchcocks. Game is so healthy—it's low in fat and cholesterol, and high in protein.

PAN FRIED DUCK BREAST WITH CARAMELISED WITLOF AND BUTTERED POTATOES

PREPARATION TIME: 20 minutes
COOKING TIME: 20 minutes
SATISFACTION VALUE: Amazed that you cooked duck!
SERVES: 2

INGREDIENTS:

40g (1$\frac{1}{3}$oz) butter
8 juniper berries
10g ($\frac{1}{3}$oz) fresh thyme
2 duck breasts (250g/8oz) each
40ml (2fl oz) madeira wine/port
200ml (6½fl oz) chicken stock

CARAMELISED WITLOF:

1 small to medium witlof
30g (1oz) butter
20g ($\frac{2}{3}$oz) brown sugar

BUTTERED POTATOES:

100g (3½oz) small potatoes
50g (1$\frac{2}{3}$oz) butter, melted

METHOD:

Let the butter warm to room temperature, then mix in the berries and thyme. Wrap the butter in plastic wrap and chuck it in the refrigerator—EASY and so cool, you can make almost any flavoured butter this way!

Preheat the oven to 200°C/400°F/gas mark 6. Score the skin of the duck breast evenly with your knife 4 or 5 times. Be careful not to cut into the meat. Season the duck breasts and pan fry in a little hot oil, skin-side down for approximately 2 minutes. Turn breasts over and continue cooking for one minute then chuck it in the hot oven for another 4 minutes.

Rest the duck for 5 minutes in a warm place. Pour madiera or port into the pan, add your stock and cook until the mixture reduces by about two-thirds. This is known as deglazing. Add the compound butter mix then pass it through a fine strainer or sieve. Serve with buttered potatoes and caramelised witlof.

CARAMELISED WITLOF:

Trim and wash witlof. Cook in simmering salted water until half cooked. Remove from water and drain on a paper towel-lined plate for a few minutes. Combine butter and brown sugar in a pan, add witlof and cook on low heat until golden brown.

BUTTERED POTATOES:

Wash and peel the potatoes. Slice into 2cm thick slices.

Preheat the oven to 250°C/485°F/gas mark 9. Grease the pan with a little butter and neatly arrange potatoes in layers, brushing with melted butter between each layer, until the pan is half full. Butter and season each layer.

Brush top with melted butter, cook on the stove for a few minutes, then transfer to the oven and cook until golden brown and crispy. Turn out of the pan and serve with the duck breast.

ROAST QUAIL WITH GRAPES AND CRANBERRY JUS

PREPARATION TIME: 20 minutes
COOKING TIME: 45 minutes
SATISFACTION VALUE: Absolutely beaut!
SERVES: 2

INGREDIENTS:

2 quail
2 slices prosciutto
4 vine leaf
salt
pepper
6 garlic cloves
100ml (3½fl oz) cranberry juice
250ml (8fl oz) chicken stock
60g (2oz) red seedless grapes
60g (2oz) butter

METHOD:

Preheat oven to 200°C/400°F/gas mark 6. Season the quails with salt and pepper. Wrap the quails with prosciutto, then the vine leaves and tie with kitchen string (you want the legs tied together). Place the quail in roasting pan with unpeeled garlic cloves and a little olive oil in the bottom of the pan. Chuck the quail into the oven and roast for 25 minutes until cooked and tender. Remove the quail and garlic from the roasting pan. Cover your quail with aluminium foil to keep it warm while you peel the garlic.

To make the sauce, place the roasting pan with the cooking juices on a high heat. Add cranberry juice, chicken stock and cook until the mixture has reduced by two-thirds. Add the peeled garlic and cook, stirring, until smooth. Strain your sauce through a sieve, pushing the garlic cloves through to extract flavour. Add the peeled and deseeded grapes to the sauce and cook for 3 minutes. Take the sauce off the heat. Add the butter, checking the seasoning and consistency.

To serve, remove the string from the quail and put on a serving platter. Spoon the sauce with grapes around the quail.

A quail is a small game bird. Think of it like a 'very very small chicken' and you will be fine. I wouldn't suggest serving this to a vegetarian or any 'hippie mates' that you might have! D'OH!

COOKING WITH LAMB

It's only in the last 50 years that people have started eating lamb. It was considered tasteless, can you believe? Crazy old people! They all preferred mutton as it was a better meat to cook with using their slow-cooking methods.

Technically, a lamb is under one year old. The younger the lamb, the more tender the meat. As a general guide when buying lamb, the darker the flesh, the older the meat. So if your butcher tells you that bright red cut there is from a six-month-old lamb, get a new butcher—young lamb should be pale pink.

CUTS OF LAMB

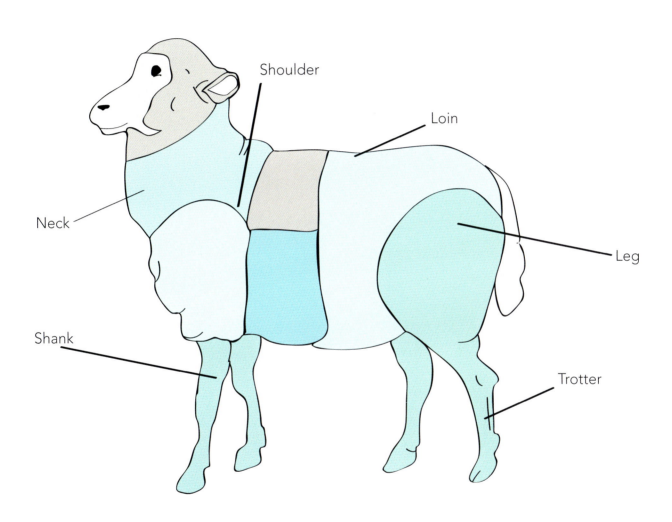

ROAST RACK OF LAMB WITH HERB CRUST

PREPARATION TIME: 20 minutes
COOKING TIME: 35 minutes
SATISFACTION VALUE: Killer
SERVES: 2

INGREDIENTS:

1 teaspoon chopped fresh mixed herbs
30g (1oz) breadcrumbs
1 teaspoon Dijon mustard
1 rack of lamb (ask your butcher to 'french trim' it for you)
20g ($2/3$oz) butter
40ml (2fl oz) stock

METHOD:

Mix your herbs with the breadcrumbs and mustard.

In a large non-stick frypan, brown the outside of the meat, then rub the herb and mustard crust onto the rack of lamb. Return the lamb to the pan and cook for approximately 15 minutes. Remove from heat and rest the lamb for 5–10 minutes.

Deglaze your pan with the stock to make the jus.

Carve the lamb and serve with either parsnip puree (from page 112) or chunky potato chips.

LAMB FILLET PASTRY WITH PARSNIP PUREE

PREPARATION TIME: 40 minutes
COOKING TIME: 40 minutes
SATISFACTION VALUE: Off the charts!
SERVES: 2

INGREDIENTS:

400g (13oz) trimmed lamb fillet
1 teaspoon tarragon
1 teaspoon chervil
1 teaspoon parsley
1 teaspoon basil
1 teaspoon thyme
salt
pepper
10g (1/3 oz) melted butter to brush over pastry to give it a nice golden brown look
2 sheets of filo pastry
50ml (1¾fl oz) red wine
50ml (1¾fl oz) brown stock
400g (13oz) parsnip, peeled and chopped roughly
200g (6½oz) potato, peeled and chopped roughly
500ml (16fl oz) milk
60g (1 2/3 oz) butter
100ml (3½fl oz) cream

METHOD:

Preheat the oven to 180°C/350°F/gas mark 4. Rub the fillet with all the herbs, then season well. Take two sheets of filo pastry, cut them each horizontally down the middle, then into three even squares.

Brush pastry with butter and lightly scrunch it into a rustic shape. Use two sheets per layer, and cook in the oven until the pastry is golden brown.

Meanwhile, make the parsnip puree by cooking the parsnip and potato in the milk until tender. Drain well. While it is still warm, mash and with a wooden spoon, push through a sieve into a bowl. Add the butter and the cream and season to taste.

Heat some butter in a pan and brown the fillet, until medium rare, take the lamb out of the oven and leave to rest for approximately five minutes.

Deglaze the pan with red wine and stock. To serve place the puree on your plate, then layer the filo pastry, followed by lamb, jus and top with second pastry piece.

STUFFED LAMB RUMP WITH RATATOUILLE AND ROCKET PESTO

PREPARATION TIME: 15 minutes
COOKING TIME: 20 minutes
SATISFACTION VALUE: Warming
SERVES: 2

INGREDIENTS:

40g (1 1/3 oz) onion, finely diced
2 garlic cloves, crushed
2 lamb rumps (300g/10oz) each
1 bunch of English spinach
40ml (1½fl oz) olive oil

RATATOUILLE:

40g (1 1/3 oz) onions
1 medium red capsicum
2 garlic cloves, peeled
1 medium zucchini
1 small eggplant

60ml (2fl oz) olive oil
30g (1oz) tomato paste
1 tomato, diced

ROCKET PESTO:

¼ bunch of rocket
30g (1oz) pine nuts
100ml (3½fl oz) virgin olive oil
60g (2oz) parmesan, grated
salt
pepper

METHOD:

First off, make the ratatouille: Chop all vegetables into 1cm (¼inch) pieces.

Heat a little oil in a frypan. Add vegetables and cook for approximately 5 minutes. Add tomato paste and diced tomato and simmer vegetables are tender. If it's a bit dry, add some water. Season to taste and set aside.

Preheat the oven to 200°C/400°F/gas mark 6. Saute onions and garlic in a frypan and set aside. Cut a pocket in the rump, fill with spinach and sautéed onions and garlic. Tie with string to enclose the filling and season well. Brown the lamb in a pan then roast in oven for approximately 12 minutes. Rest the lamb for five minutes then make a jus from the pan juices. Serve on the ratatouille.

For the rocket pesto, whiz all the ingredients in a food processor until well blended. It may be necessary to scrape the sides down a couple of times. Serve the rump on top of the ratatouille with the rocket pesto around the edge of the plate for garnish.

Unused pesto will keep, refrigerated, for about a week.

LEMON SOUFFLÉ

PREPARATION TIME: 10 minutes
COOKING TIME: 20 minutes
SATISFACTION VALUE: If you nail it you will love it!
SERVES: 2

INGREDIENTS:

200ml (6½fl oz) milk
¼ vanilla pod
3 egg yolks
60g (2oz) caster sugar
20g (²/₃oz) flour
1 whole lemon, juice and zest

SOUFFLE:

1 teaspoon butter
caster sugar (for sprinkling inside moulds)
2 egg whites

METHOD:

To make pastry cream, bring the milk and vanilla to the boil in a saucepan. Whisk egg yolks and sugar in a bowl until almost white, then mix in your flour. Pour milk into egg mixture while whisking. Transfer the mixture into a clean pan, and bring to the boil while stirring. Remove from the heat, add lemon juice and zest and cool. Sprinkle with sugar and set aside until needed.

Preheat oven to 200°C/400°F/gas mark 6. Grease two ramekins with butter and sprinkle with sugar. Whisk the egg whites to firm peaks and gently fold into pastry cream in two stages. This helps ensure maximum air-retention.

Pour mixture into the ramekins and chuck them in the oven for 10–15 minutes. Dust with sugar to serve.

For this recipe you will need individual soufflé dishes known as ramekins..

BREAD AND BUTTER PUDDING

PREPARATION TIME: 15 minutes
COOKING TIME: 50 minutes
SATISFACTION VALUE: Feels like home
SERVES: 2–4 depending on size of dishes.

INGREDIENTS:

For this recipe you will require some small cake moulds or as they're technically known 'dariole moulds. If you really want to, you can use a big pie dish.
4 slices of bread
80g (2 $\frac{2}{3}$oz) butter
2 eggs
60g (2oz) sugar
500ml (16fl oz) milk
½ teaspoon vanilla essence
40g (1$\frac{1}{3}$oz) sultanas
pinch of nutmeg

METHOD:

Lightly grease your moulds or pie dish.

Butter both sides of the bread. Cut the crusts off then cut the slices into triangles.

Whisk eggs and sugar together until white and fluffy, then stir in milk and vanilla essence.

Preheat oven to 180°C/350°F/gas mark 4. Line the dishes with buttered bread then sprinkle over the sultanas. Pour the egg, milk and sugar mix over the bread. Sprinkle with nutmeg.

Place your dish or moulds into a roasting pan and pour enough boiling water in the roasting pan that it comes half way up the dishes or moulds.

Cover moulds with foil and bake for 15 minutes. Then remove foil and bake for another 15 minutes.

I can officially say I hate winter! Not only is the water bloody cold but that wicked summer vibe has disappeared for another three months. These recipes are good to warm you up at home in front of the heater or under the blanket. I reckon slow-cooked hot dishes are ideal for the winter months. There is nothing better than inviting a girl around and serving some real fit, delicious food. These recipes are easy and will make your house smell great.

Braising is half covering food (usually meat) in liquid and cooked slowly in a tight-lidded container. The cooking liquid is usually used as a sauce at the end.

The great thing about braising is that you can afford to use the cheaper cuts of meat. This means you will have a killer meal without breaking the budget. Shanks, for example, are really cheap but so tasty and impressive when you cook them. Ask your butcher for cheap cuts and replace the cuts in each recipe.

WINTER WARMERS

BRAISED OXTAIL WITH GREEN BEANS

PREPARATION TIME: 30 minutes
COOKING TIME: 3½ hours
SATISFACTION VALUE: Wicked
SERVES: 2

INGREDIENTS:

1kg (2lb) oxtail
50ml (1¾fl oz) oil
1 small onion, chopped coarsely
1 small stalk celery, chopped coarsely
1 small carrot, chopped coarsely
60g (2oz) flour
25g (¾oz) tomato paste
500ml (16fl oz) stock
30ml (1fl oz) red wine
1 bay leaf
50g (1⅔oz) green beans
1 tablespoon butter

METHOD:

Cut the oxtail into sections and remove excess fat. Alternatively, ask your butcher to prep it for you. Fry meat on all sides in hot fat then transfer to braising pan or casserole dish.

Add onion, garlic, celery and carrot to the pot and cook until brown.

Mix in your flour, add your tomato paste, stock, red wine, salt and pepper and a bay leaf. Bring to the boil and skim the fat off the top. Cover and simmer in oven until tender for approximately 3 hours.

Remove the oxtail from the sauce, place in a clean pan, correct the consistency of the sauce and seasoning, pass the sauce through a sieve and place over the meat and bring to the boil again (the meat can be picked off the bone if you want before serving if you have fussy people coming for dinner.) Place the green beans in a pot with boiling water and butter. Cover and set aside for 5 minutes or until beans are tender.

Again, oxtail is so cheap ... but great tasting!

BEEF BOURGUIGNON WITH WICKED MASH

PREPARATION TIME: 15 minutes
COOKING TIME: 2½ hours
SATISFACTION VALUE: Sorted
SERVES: 2

INGREDIENTS:

400g (13½oz) beef, diced
1 small onion, chopped roughly
75g (2½oz) bacon
30g (1oz) flour
25ml (1$\frac{1}{3}$fl oz) olive oil
20g ($\frac{2}{3}$oz) tomato paste
650ml (21fl oz) beef stock
150ml (5½fl oz) red wine
1 bay leaf
1 garlic clove
1 small carrot, chopped into pieces
1 small stalk celery, chopped into pieces

25g (1oz) leek, sliced thickly
100g (3½oz) mushrooms
3–4 shallots, chopped
chopped parsley

WICKED MASH:

3 potatoes, peeled and chopped into small pieces
150ml (5½ fl oz) cream
150g (5oz) butter
salt
pepper

METHOD:

Preheat oven to 180°C/350°F/gas mark 4. Season the beef with salt and pepper. Quickly fry the meat in a little oil until brown. Add onion, bacon and flour and cook til it becomes really sticky. This should take about 3 minutes. Stir in tomato paste and cook for another 30 seconds then add your stock, red wine, bay leaf and garlic. Bring to the boil. Skim the fat off the top of the sauce and cover. Add carrot, celery, leek, mushrooms and shallots. Cook in oven until tender, about 1½–2 hours.

Transfer the meat and vegetables onto a serving plate. Correct your sauce by adding seasoning. Pass the sauce through a sieve on to your meat. Serve with Wicked Mash and garnish with parsley!

WICKED MASH:

In a large saucepan or pot, cover potatoes with salted water and bring to a boil. Boil for 20 minutes or until fluffy and soft.

Meanwhile, in a separate pan, heat cream and butter in the pan until the butter melts into the cream.

Once the potatoes are cooked, strain them, place them back into the pot, and slowly start to mash them up while adding the cream mixture. Mash with a masher until smooth. The more liquid you put in, the easier and smoother the mash. Season with heaps of salt and pepper.

BRAISED LAMB SHANKS WITH RICE PILAF

PREPARATION TIME: 45 minutes
COOKING TIME: 3 hours
SATISFACTION VALUE: Succulent
SERVES: 2

INGREDIENTS:

2 lamb shanks
25g (1oz) flour, seasoned with salt and pepper
1 onion, chopped coarsely
1 carrot, chopped coarsely
1 stalk celery, chopped coarsely
2 garlic cloves
1 sprig rosemary
1 teaspoon dried oregano
50g (1^2/$_3$oz) tomato paste
10ml (½fl oz) red wine vinegar
500ml (16fl oz) beef stock
2 tomatoes
20ml (1fl oz) olive oil
1 bay leaf

BRAISED RICE PILAF:

50g (1^2/$_3$oz) butter
25g (1oz) chopped onion
100g (3½oz) long grain rice
150ml (5¼fl oz) chicken stock

METHOD:

Preheat the oven to 180°C/350°F/gas mark 4. Dust your lamb shanks in seasoned flour, then heat some oil in a frypan and brown the shanks. Remove the shanks and set aside. Add your onion, carrot and celery to the oil and cook until golden brown. Add garlic, herbs and tomato paste and cook for one minute further on low heat.

Add the vinegar and stock and bring to the boil. Return the lamb shanks to the pot. Add the whole tomatoes and bay leaf. Cover with foil and cook in the oven for 2½ hours. Remove the lamb shanks. Pass the remainder of the sauce through a sieve into a separate pot. Correct seasoning and consistency. Serve with rice pilaf.

BRAISED RICE PILAF:

Preheat the oven to 200°C/400°F/gas mark 6. Place half the butter in a small pan, add the onion and cook on low heat for 2–3 minutes. Add the rice, mix well, then add stock.

Cover with greaseproof baking paper and bring to the boil. Place in oven for 15 minutes until rice is cooked. Mix in the remaining butter with a fork.

THE BEEF ON BEEF

Beef is so tasty and versatile—it can be used for stews, casseroles, curries and roasts. But my favourite way to have beef is just chucking a good steak on the barbecue. When your friends want their steaks 'medium rare', don't freak out, just follow these basic guidelines:

- Rare steak will be soft and squishy when you press it with tongs
- Medium-rare steak will be soft but not squishy
- Medium steak will be just firm
- Medium to well done steak will be slightly firm but not hard
- Well-done steak will be hard. Unless your friend likes their steak this way, I wouldn't advise cooking a steak to well done!

CUTS OF BEEF

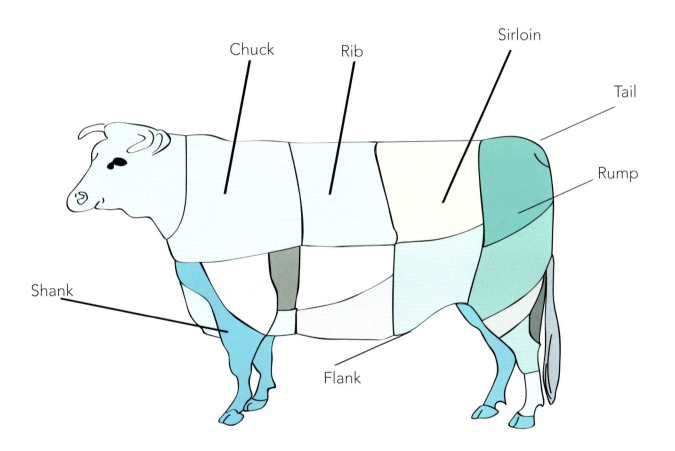

Right. You've met her, you've been out once or twice and now you've invited her to your place for dinner. Daunting or what? Don't worry, these recipes are smooth and straightforward. Not only that, they're well impressive.

ROMANTIC DINNERS

MUSSELS WITHOUT THINKING

PREPARATION TIME: 15 minutes
COOKING TIME: 20 minutes
SERVES: 2

INGREDIENTS:

1 tablespoon vegetable oil
1 onion, sliced
6 garlic cloves, crushed
1 capsicum, sliced
2 chillies, chopped finely
2kg (4lb) mussels
100ml (3½fl oz) white wine
1 can of peeled tomatoes
100ml (3½fl oz) cream
salt
pepper

METHOD:

Heat the oil in a big pot. Add onion, garlic and capsicum and to the oil. Cook on low heat. Add chopped chilli and your mussels and mix it all up.

Pour in white wine and canned tomatoes. Stir, then cover with a lid. Cook on a medium heat for about 10 minutes or until the mussels open. Discard any that don't open after about 15 minutes of cooking.

Stir again and then add your cream to finish. Do a taste test and add salt and pepper as required. Serve with nice, crusty bread to soak up the sauce.

This is by far the best mussel dish. You can eat it in many different ways, either with the shells in the bowl and some bread, or how I love it, taking the mussels out of their shells after the dish has been served so I'm left with a big bowl of broth and mussels, like a mussel soup—its seriously bleeping nice!

SIMPLE AND EASY LAMB CUTLETS

PREPARATION TIME: 10 minutes
COOKING TIME: 5 minutes
SERVES: 2

INGREDIENTS:

8 lamb cutlets
salt
pepper
1 tablespoon olive oil
30ml (1fl oz) balsamic vinegar

METHOD:

Season lamb cutlets well with salt and pepper. Heat a non-stick frypan on high heat until the pan is hot then add the oil.

Place your lamb cutlets into the pan. Cook for a minute and a half on each side, until the lamb has changed colour.

Add the balsamic vinegar—this will caramelise over the top of the lamb cutlets. Remove cutlets from heat and leave to rest for 5 minutes before serving. I love serving these with a simple salad, like the rocket and witlof (see Sunday Barbecues).

MAKING YOUR GIRLFRIEND HAPPY

- Toast each other when you sit down to dinner. Tell her something you love about her and then drink to it!

- Use the power of touch. There is no such thing as not having time for a kiss goodbye in the morning or an inviting warm hug or backrub at the end of a stressful day.

- Do something thoughtful for her every day. Whether it's making her a cup of coffee in the morning, sticking a surprise note in her bag, or leaving her a chocolate "kiss" on her pillow before bedtime, everyone loves a romantic surprise.

- Let her see you at your best.

- Tell her you couldn't have done it without her. Whether it's the birthday party she planned or just a supermarket run, let her know she's important to you, and you're grateful.

- Tell her that she is your ideal-looking woman. She probably won't believe you, but she will still feel sexy hearing it and who knows what will happen then!

- Whether it's trouble at the office or a T-shirt purchase, if you ask her opinion she'll think you care about what she thinks. The ladies love you liking their brain as well as their bodies.

- If you tell a girl that you think your family would adore her, you are guaranteed a big smile.

- Tell her she's gorgeous regularly. There's not a girl who doesn't want to feel beautiful. If she feels stunning in your eyes, she'll let you gaze away, even at the parts she'd normally hide.

BOBBY'S CRÈME BRULEE

PREPARATION TIME: 10 minutes
COOKING TIME: 30 minutes
SERVES: 4

INGREDIENTS:

625ml (20fl oz) thickened cream
½ teaspoon vanilla essence or
1 whole vanilla bean (if you want to go all gourmet)
8 egg yolks
3 tablespoons caster sugar
1 punnet of strawberries
Some brown sugar if you have a blow torch and want to caramelise the tops of the Brulee.

METHOD:

Right, grab either one big dish or 4 nice glasses or ramekins. Place them in the refrigerator to cool.

In a pan on low heat, slowly warm the cream. Add in your vanilla essence (if you have a vanilla bean, then carefully open the bean up and scrape the seeds into the cream using a knife).

While the cream is heating up, whisk the egg yolks in a mixing bowl. Whisk in the sugar until the mixture has doubled in size and looks all white and creamy. (A tip—sit the mixing bowl on top of a folded tea towel to stop it sliding around.)

When the cream has boiled, turn the heat off and let the cream cool down (if you have put the whole vanilla bean in as well as the seeds, then take the bloody thing out now before we choke someone!)

Now pour the cream into your egg and sugar mixture and whisk it all together. Wait until it has all combined and a lot of little bubbles have formed.

Now return the mixture to the pan on low heat. Gently stir it continuously for about 10 minutes. The mixture will slowly start to thicken. When it gets to a consistency where it coats the back of your wooden spoon and all the bubbles have gone from the surface then the mixture is ready.

Pour the mixture into your serving dish or dishes. I like to slice the strawberries and pop them into the dish before we pour the mixture in, but this is optional. Chuck them into the refrigerator and let it set. It should take a few hours.

Once set, you can either put brown sugar over the top and use a flame to create caramel for a great crunch, or just put freshly sliced strawberries neatly over the top and serve.

IT'S WELL FIT!

Crème Brulee is one of my favourite desserts, I love it and after you try this so will you!

VALENTINE'S DAY

Valentine's Day… mmm … not my favourite day in the calendar year, but unfortunately it is important to most girls. Although they'll say it's not, trust me—it is.

These dishes will ensure you have a successful Valentine's Day, but also have to follow these few simple rules:

1. Girls over-analyse EVERYTHING. So if you're playing romantic music in the background, make sure it doesn't have any words, as they'll think you are saying all that to them. (Crazy I know, but true!)

2. Don't go nuts on the décor, but make a clear effort. Tea lights in short drinking glasses are so effective and cost bugger all.

3. When you are interacting with your guest, make sure you ask lots of questions about her, and always listen. (Try not to tune out in case she asks you a question back!)

4. DON'T DRINK TOO MUCH. Have enough water available so you don't get smashed. A loose first date will not lead to another date, especially if you're the loose one.

CHAMPAGNE COCKTAIL

PREPARATION TIME: 5 minutes
SATISFACTION VALUE: Bubbling all night long
SERVES: 6

INGREDIENTS:

6 sugar cubes
Angostura bitters, to taste
30ml (1 1/3 fl oz) brandy
750ml (24fl oz) Champagne or sparkling wine, chilled

METHOD:

Place a sugar cube in each of the Champagne glasses. Drizzle with 4–5 drops of bitters and set aside for 5 minutes to soak.

Pour brandy evenly among glasses and top with Champagne or sparkling wine.

Serve immediately.

Bubbles to start off with will set you up well. You won't need to buy an expensive bottle, a good cheap one will do.

CRISPY-SKIN OCEAN TROUT WITH CAULIFLOWER PUREE

PREPARATION TIME: 20 minutes
COOKING TIME: 20 minutes
SATISFACTION VALUE: Fit
SERVES: 2

INGREDIENTS:

1 cauliflower, cut into florets
1L (32fl oz) milk
2 bay leaves
30ml (1 1/3 fl oz) extra virgin olive oil
20g (2/3 oz) butter
2 x 125g (4oz) ocean trout fillets
salt
pepper
1 lemon

METHOD:

Make the puree first by combining cauliflower, milk and some water in a large saucepan. Add bay leaves and bring to the boil. Reduce heat and simmer for 25–30 minutes until cauliflower is tender. Strain cauliflower from milk, reserve milk and remove bay leaves.

Transfer cauliflower to a food processor, add a little of the reserved milk. Season lightly and puree. Add just enough milk to attain a soft mashed-potato-like consistency. Set aside and reheat in a frypan on low heat, or in the microwave just before serving.

Heat a large non-stick frypan over a medium heat. Add 10ml of olive oil and butter, heat until the butter starts to sizzle. Season the fillets well, and place skin-side-down into the pan. Move the fish around slightly to ensure it is not stuck. If you want to you can add more oil but be careful because the oil will spit if it gets too hot.

When the middle of the fillet starts getting pale, turn it over and start cooking the other side. This should take no longer than 5 minutes. The fish should take 10 minutes on the heat and 5 minutes resting to be 'medium'. If you want it 'well done' you should cook it for a further 5 minutes in the pan. Remember you can always preheat your oven to 180°C/350°F/gas mark 4 and finish the fish in there for 10 minutes or so.

I like to serve this dish with the olive oil and lemon juice whisked up to make a dressing.

With the bright pink of the ocean trout and the white, creamy cauliflour, it will POP from the plate.

VANILLA PANACOTTA WITH CHOCOLATE SAUCE

PREPARATION TIME: 15 minutes
COOKING TIME: 15 minutes
SATISFACTION VALUE: yummy
SERVES: 4

INGREDIENTS:

½ a vanilla bean
250ml (8fl oz) cream
5g (1/6oz) leaf gelatine
40g (1 1/3oz) caster sugar
50g (1 1/3oz) milk chocolate buttons

METHOD:

Split the vanilla bean and scrape the seeds into a saucepan on low heat. Add 200ml (6fl oz) of the cream and bring to the boil. Meanwhile, soak gelatine in cold water until it's soft, then drain.

Add your sugar and soft gelatine to hot cream. Mix it all together then strain mixture through a sieve.

Divide mixture between 4 plastic moulds, cover each mould and refrigerate for two hours.

For the chocolate sauce, heat the remaining cream but not to boiling point. Add the chocolate and whisk until combined.

To serve, dip your moulds into warm water and turn them out on to plates. You may need to help release them with a small knife.

This dish is said to be hard, but I disagree. As long as you leave enough time for it to set you will be fine. Morning or night before is ideal.

A night in with the lads, some sport and a few drinks is always great fun. I love sharing a great big bowl of curry with my mates and all tucking in whilst we argue about sport, girls and video games!

FRIDAY NIGHT WITH THE BOYS

POTATO WEDGES WITH CHILLI AND GARLIC AIOLI

PREPARATION TIME: 15 minutes
COOKING TIME: 20 minutes
SERVES: 4

INGREDIENTS:

4 potatoes (medium-sized Pontiac)
4 garlic cloves
3 eggs
20ml (1fl oz) white vinegar
1 teaspoon mustard
salt
pepper
250ml (8fl oz) oil

METHOD:

Preheat the oven to 180°C/350°/gas mark 4. Cut your potatoes into wedges and put them in a saucepan with enough water to cover them. Add a pinch of salt and boil them until the potatoes are just soft. Then strain well. (You can keep these in the refrigerator for up to a week if you want to be really prepared!).

Meanwhile, make the aioli by roasting your garlic in the oven, checking every five minutes until it's soft in the middle. While it's roasting, break two eggs into the food processor and add one more egg yolk. Add the white vinegar, mustard, salt and pepper to taste and whiz it together. Slowly add the oil until it becomes nice and thick.

Peel the roasted garlic and add that and the mayo and whiz once more. You can correct the consistency of your aioli with a tiny bit of boiling water and then season it to taste. That's easy aioli!

You can either cook the potatoes in the oven or make your own deep fryer on the stove top with a few cups of sunflower oil in a pot. Deep frying is not for the faint-hearted. Minimise the risk by keeping your distance to avoid spitting.

To bake: Preheat the oven to 195°C/380°F/gas mark 5. Toss the wedges in oil and roast them in the oven for 15–20 minutes until golden brown.

To serve, season with salt and dish them out in a nice big bowl with the aioli on the side.

SPICY VINDALOO

PREPARATION TIME: 15 minutes
COOKING TIME: 2.5 hrs
SERVES: 4

INGREDIENTS:

30ml (1 1/3fl oz) oil
10g (1/3oz) curry powder
10g (1/3oz) chopped ginger
1 teaspoon ground fennel seeds
1 teaspoon ground cumin
1 teaspoon ground cardamom
1 teaspoon cayenne pepper
500g (1lb) diced lamb
15g (½oz) vindaloo paste (any brand will do)
100g (3½oz) chopped onions
10g (1/3oz) tomato paste
10g (1/3oz) flour
20ml (1fl oz) natural yoghurt

METHOD:

If you're using whole spices, to make sure the flavours really explode, you'll need to grind them down using a mortar and pestle—just throw them in and mash them all up! To save time, get all your ingredients chopped and separated before you start cooking.

Heat the oil in a large pan, throw in your spices and cook on low heat until fragrant. Add your lamb and brown the meat. Now we give the dish another flavour hit—in goes the vindaloo paste! Mix this in for a couple of minutes.

Add onions and continue cooking for 2–3 minutes on medium heat. Give your curry some real body with tomato paste and flour and continue stirring on medium heat until well combined.

Add 500ml (16fl oz) water, turn the stove up to high and bring to the boil. Turn back down to low heat and simmer for an hour and a half or until your meat is tender.

You know it's ready to go if the sauce is reduced to a coating consistency, so then turn off the heat and finish by adding yoghurt. I always serve this dish with some rice pilaf or steamed rice.

If you like your curry to pack a real bang, make it hotter by adding a couple of chopped chillies at the beginning.

THAI GREEN CURRY

PREPARATION TIME: 20 minutes
COOKING TIME: 45 minutes
SERVES: 4

INGREDIENTS:

2cm (¾inch) ginger, diced finely
handful coriander
1 clove garlic
250g (8oz) chicken breast
150g (5oz) chicken leg meat off the bone
20ml (1fl oz) peanut oil
1 teaspoon green thai curry paste
2 small red chillies, chopped roughly
1 onion, diced finely
5cm (2inch) piece lemon grass, chopped finely
2 kaffir lime leaves
1 star anise
10g (⅓oz) palm sugar
2 drops fish sauce
handful sweet Thai basil (use basil if Thai basil isn't available)
150ml (5½fl oz) coconut cream

METHOD:

Again for this curry, you'll be on easy street if you prep the ingredients before you start cooking.

Chop up the ginger, coriander and garlic into small pieces. A good tip for the garlic is to crush the peeled clove with the back of your knife before chopping it. This makes the chopping easier and the flavour explode!

Remove any skin on the chicken—just get in there and rip it off!

Heat the oil in a pan over a medium heat. Add the curry paste and fry for a couple of minutes or until the aromas start filling your kitchen. Now add your chillies, onion, ginger, garlic coriander and lemongrass.

Chuck in the chicken and cook for 4 minutes until browned. Add the rest of your ingredients, stirring through until well combined and simmer over a low heat for 20 minutes.

To serve, I like to put out a big bowl of rice topped with chopped coriander leaves and another big bowl for the curry. This saves you from serving up and lets the boys tuck in and have what they want—probably a truckload!

GUYS GUIDE TIPS

- You can't soar with the eagles if you spend your time hanging with the chickens.

- Find people who are going where you want to go, and 'conspire to aspire before you expire'.

- Atmosphere is critical, diligently guard who enters your inner-circle.

- Your friends are a prophecy of your future.

- It sounds simple, but many people live a life of repeating the same mistakes over and over again. The "cow in the ditch" example below gives us a pattern for how we should deal with our mistakes.

- Here are the three steps you should follow whenever a cow ends up in your ditch.

    Step 1:   Get Cow Out of Ditch

    Step 2:   Find Out How Cow Got in Ditch

    Step 3:   Make Sure Cow Does Not Get in Ditch Again

- Eat breakfast daily. Breakfast flips on your metabolism like a furnace switch, so your body fires up and starts burning calories. I recommend a carbohydrates-protein combo. On Sunday nights, I premix yogurt, oats and berries, and store them, refrigerated in a container for five days' worth of quick breakfasts.

- Drink water all day. Before lunch, neck 350ml of water. We often feel hungry when we're just dehydrated. Be that geek with the reusable water bottle at the desk, at least you'll be fit!

OK, we've all had a hangover. What you need to do is prepare your body for the hangover and make it the easiest process ever. Guys, don't just get home from a night out, open a beer and pass out on the sofa (I did this for years). You don't need that beer or glass of wine when you get home, just grab a massive bottle of water from your refrigerator (the one you filled before you went out!) and drink that. Then go to sleep and take it easy the next day!

HANGOVER CURES

BEST AND CLEANEST SCRAMBLED EGG FRY-UP

PREPARATION TIME: 10 minutes
COOKING TIME: 15 minutes
SATISFACTION VALUE: NO washing up!
SERVES: 1

INGREDIENTS:

3 rashers of bacon
1 tomato
1 slice of bread
3 eggs
20ml (1fl oz) milk
10g ($1/_3$oz) butter
handful of chives

METHOD:

Because you're hungover, we'll cheat!

Turn the grill on and grab a baking tray. Cover the tray in foil, lay your three rashers of bacon on the foil. Slice your tomato in half and season with salt and pepper. Place next to bacon.

Put your bread into the toaster and pop your oven tray under the grill and remember to leave it slightly open. Turn your bacon after around 3 minutes or so

For the scrambled eggs, whisk up 3 eggs in any kind of leftover takeaway container until completely combined. Mix in the milk and a lump of butter. Season with salt and pepper. Cook in microwave for 20 seconds. Take the mix out and stir again. At this stage the butter should be almost melted and the eggs half cooked. Keep repeating this process until you reach the desired consistency.

Sprinkle chopped chives through the egg mix and serve on the top of toast.

By this stage your bacon and tomato should be nicely toasted. Pull out, whack it on a plate and enjoy. Chuck the foil and plastic container in the bin and you're done. Cleaning up has never been easier!

SCHNITZEL AND POTATO ROSTI WITH MUSHROOM SAUCE

PREPARATION TIME: 20 minutes
COOKING TIME: 20 minutes
SATISFACTION VALUE: Worth the effort
SERVES: 1

INGREDIENTS:

250g (8oz) potatoes
120g (3¾oz) chicken or veal fillet
100g (3½oz) flour
150g (5oz) breadcrumbs
1 egg, lightly beaten
75g (2½oz) butter
1 lemon
25g (¾oz) chopped parsley

MUSHROOM SAUCE:

2 tablespoons butter
2 garlic cloves, crushed
200g (6½oz) button mushrooms, chopped
2 teaspoons of Dijon mustard
235ml (7½oz) pouring cream
1 teaspoon mixed herbs dried for seasoning
salt
pepper

METHOD:

Boil the potatoes in their skins until they are ¾ cooked.

Meanwhile, wrap your chicken or veal in plastic wrap. Place on a chopping board and bash it with a rolling pin or cricket bat (careful you don't bash too hard!) until it is flat and the size you require.

Place the flour on to a small plate, breadcrumbs on another and the beaten egg in a bowl.

Coat the flattened veal or chicken in the flour, then dip it in the beaten egg and coat in breadcrumbs.

Heat one-third of the butter in a pan and cook the schnitzel for a few minutes on each side.

Remove the skins of the potatoes with a paring knife and grate the potatoes on the coarse grater. Heat butter in a frypan and cook grated potato with some salt and pepper until golden brown. Add more butter if necessary. Turn over and cook the other side until golden brown.

Serve with schnitzel.

MUSHROOM SAUCE:

Melt the butter in the pan with the garlic, add the mushrooms and cook until the butter is all absorbed. Season the mushrooms with salt and pepper.

You can add a splash of white wine at this stage if you have it lying around. Only a splash though! Add the mustard, cream and sprinkle some mixed herbs over the top.

Stir until thick and serve. Seriously easy and well nice!

CHOCOLATE THICK SHAKE

PREPARATION TIME: 5 minutes
SATISFACTION VALUE: WELL FIT!
SERVES: 1

INGREDIENTS:

3 big scoops of chocolate or vanilla ice-cream
3 tablespoons drinking chocolate
half a banana
350ml (11½fl oz) milk

METHOD:

Whiz all ingredients in a blender and pour into a chilled glass. This will give you the best sugar hit ever.

FISH FINGER SANDWICH WITH AIOLI

PREPARATION TIME: 10 minutes
COOKING TIME: 15 minutes
SATISFACTION VALUE: Just what the doctor ordered
SERVES: 1–2

INGREDIENTS:

4 fish fingers
2 slices of bread
aioli or good quality mayonnaise
1 hash brown
handful of rocket leaves
tomato sauce (optional)

METHOD:

Cook fish fingers according to packet directions until golden and crispy. Spread aioli on one slice of the bread, top with rocket leaves and fish fingers then add the final finishing touch … a hash brown!

You can add some tomato sauce, which I like to do. It somehow creates this thousand island sauce mix, which just tastes wicked at 3am!

I love these, I really do. Fish fingers always hit the spot. Also it's so much better to get home after a night out and offer a friend a fish finger sandwich, than to get a kebab and have it running down your chin and shirt, and have you stinking of garlic and chilli sauce.

MASHED BANANA AND ICE CREAM

PREPARATION TIME: 5 minutes
COOKING TIME: 5 minutes
SATISFACTION VALUE: Naughty but very nice
SERVES: 2

INGREDIENTS:

2 bananas
20g (2/3oz) butter
10g (1/3oz) brown sugar
200g (6½oz) vanilla ice cream

METHOD:

Peel your bananas and mash in a microwave-safe bowl. Top with the butter and sugar then heat them in the microwave for up to 2 minutes. Remove and mash some more.

Serve piping hot with a huge dollop of vanilla ice cream on top!

This will sort your hangover out. I love it with chocolate sauce over the top as well.

CHOCOLATE SAUCE:

200g (6½oz) chocolate buttons
100ml (3½fl oz) of cream

Heat the cream on the stove in a pan and add the chocolate buttons. Stir until chocolate is melted. Use a gentle heat so as to not burn the chocolate. This is well fit!

   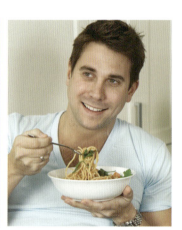

What's the best scenario when you're ill? To eat well and get better ASAP, but pretend to be sick and keep getting pampered by the missus!

Here are some simple rules to follow when you're ill:

- Go to bed early and cover up
- Rub vapourrub on your chest, back and just under your nose before you hit the sack (this will help you sleep)
- Drink lots of fluids—cordials are great for rebuilding body sugars
- Drink lots of hot water or tea with lemon and honey,
- Don't drink alcohol and for God's sake, don't smoke. Give it up for one week and you will be fine.
- Eat as many healthy foods as you can—that's right—veggies!

FEELING ILL

CHICKEN AND POTATO SOUP

PREPARATION TIME: 20 minutes
COOKING TIME: 2 hours
SERVES: 4

INGREDIENTS:

1 whole chicken
10g ($1/3$oz) parsely
2 garlic cloves
100ml ($3 1/3$oz) white wine
2 onions
4 potatoes, peeled and chopped into chunks
salt
pepper

METHOD:

Put the chicken into a big pot and cover with water. Roughly chop one of the onions and throw in the pot. Bring this to the boil, then reduce heat and cover. Simmer for 45 minutes.

Turn off the heat and rest the chicken for 40 minutes. Then remove the chicken, and there will be beautiful chicken broth remaining.

Fry off the other chopped onion, garlic until softened, add the chopped potato and mix to heat the potato up, add the wine and stir. Now add the chicken broth, pop the lid back and bring back to the boil. Reduce heat and simmer for 20–25 minutes.

While this is bubbling away, peel the skin off the chicken and shred the meat with your fingers—you'll find the bird will be fall apart in your hands. Once the chicken is all shredded, set it aside.

Whiz everything in the pot together in a blender or food processor to make a nice thick soup. Don't forget to season with salt and pepper! Throw in the shredded chicken, give it a stir and garnish with some chopped parsley.

GRANDMA'S 'BUNG IN' SOUP POEM

My grandma wrote me this poem so I would never forget this soup. This soup is a killer, it's bloody wicked. I also love to put a spoonful of baked beans in when I serve it. Hence, my nickname as a kid was 'Baked Bean Bobby'.

To start you need a big round pot,
And in it a potato,
then give it lots of glow with
a big round red tomato.

Another main ingredient is
a good strong, healthy onion.
Do not throw the skin away,
but rub it on your bunion.

Then you want a carrot too
and that's the final need,
But also for some thickness,
you really need a swede!

And now to really start the fun
you bung in this and that,
whatever you can find around,
but not a precious cat.

You look into your cupboard store
and find some nice split peas,
you throw in quite a handful,
but not too many please.
Now if you cannot find these things,
I'm sure you've got some lentils,
For they will do you just as well.

The other things that work as well,
are celery, leeks and cabbage.
But do not put anything cooked,
as the brew will taste of garbage.

Now don't forget the final bit,
you need a nice strong flavour.
You need 3 pints of made up stock,
and that will be your saviour.

You now must cook the whole darn lot,
by pressure gas or electric.
I don't know how much time to give,
As I've never managed metric.

When the veg are cooked and blended,
then you think your work is done,
oh dear me it hasn't ended
How the fun has just begun!

Now you have to liquidise it,
put in spoonfuls of the brew.
Once I told you how to do this,
and you souped the ceiling too.

If you've done what I have told you
you can give a joyful woop!
Then you've got a Christmas present,
Bowls of Grandma's bung-in soup.
~ Grandma 2008

So what my Grandma was really saying is: Bung a whole heap of vegetables in a pot and cook for about 30 minutes on medium heat, until all the ingredients are soft. Add 3 pints (1.5L/48fl oz) of stock then blend it until smooth in a food processor or blender. I love this with thick crunchy bread and a dollop of baked beans in the middle!

BOBBY'S BOLOGNESE

PREPARATION TIME: 30 minutes
COOKING TIME: 1 hour
SERVES: 4–6

INGREDIENTS:

1 brown onion
1 red onion
1 bunch of basil
4 garlic cloves
2 chillies
1 carrot
1 tablespoon olive oil
1 bay leaf
Some dried oregano leaves
1kg (2lb) premium beef mince
1 x 420g (13 2/3 oz) can of Italian peeled tomatoes
1 bottle (750ml/24fl oz) of red wine
1 jar of Bolognese sauce, any brand will do
2 tomatoes, diced
60g (2oz) tomato paste
2 teaspoons Worcestershire sauce
2 teaspoons balsamic vinegar
Salt
Pepper
500g dried pasta
parmesan cheese, to serve

METHOD:

Finely dice onions and chop the basil (put some basil aside for garnish). Finely chop the garlic, chilli and carrots—make your carrots about the same size as the onion.

Season with salt and pepper. Put the olive oil in a pan (quite a big pan for the 1kg of mince!) and turn stove up to high. Add your onions, garlic and chilli. Stir until onion softens.

Now throw in the bay leaf and dried oregano while the onion sweats.

Add your mince to the pot and cook until brown, then in go the olives. Add a can of peeled tomatoes and the whole bottle of red wine (or just half and you can drink the rest with dinner!)

Stir in the jar of bolognese sauce and cook for 15 minutes. Throw the fresh tomatoes and the tomato paste in there too. Give it all a stir and leave to boil. Turn down the heat, add the Worcestershire sauce and balsamic vinegar. Simmer for another 10 minutes. Taste and adjust the seasoning!

Meanwhile, cook the pasta in boiling water according to packet directions—you can use any pasta you like, spirals, penne, or my favourite—good ol' spaghetti. Serve garnished with the chopped basil that you set aside earlier and the parmesan cheese.

Make up a massive batch of this and freeze it so you can keep having it, week in week out! Trust me it's a winner!

LEMON TART

PREPARATION TIME: 15 minutes
COOKING TIME: 45 minutes
SERVES: 4

INGREDIENTS:

3 eggs
110g (3¾oz) caster sugar
1 lemon (juice and zest)
100ml (3½fl oz) cream
30ml (1⅓fl oz) double cream
1 tart shell (about 18cm/7inches wide)

METHOD:

Preheat the oven to 140°C/275°F/gas mark 1–2. In a large bowl, mix eggs and sugar with an electric mixer until light and fluffy, then stir in lemon juice and cream. Add the zest and mix well to combine

Pour into pastry case and cook in oven, checking every 10 minutes until filling is set. Remember to turn the dish now and then to even out the cooking. Serve at room temperature, sprinkled with sifted icing sugar and a fat dollop of double cream.

I love tarts! ;-) (...such a dad joke, but a goodie!)

You don't have to go out to have a celebration. Make some cocktails, invite everyone round to your place and turn on the stereo (don't forget to let the neighbours know otherwise they'll be cranky). And the best part? There's no cab fare home!

PARTY TIME!

SANGRIA

PREPARATION TIME: 2 minutes
SATISFACTION VALUE: Feel Spanish!
SERVES: 4

INGREDIENTS:

You need a massive jug or bowl for this to go in!
750ml (24fl oz) red wine
450ml (14½fl oz) apple juice (sparkling if you can get it)
200ml (6½fl oz) orange juice
60ml (2fl oz) vodka
60ml (2fl oz) gin
1 orange, sliced into circles
20ml (1fl oz) fresh lemon juice
1 lime, cut into slices
1 apple, cut into chunks

METHOD:

Combine all ingredients with ice in your massive jug. Then smash it up! To chill, you can put in the refrigerator.

For those of you who haven't tried Sangria before—this will get any party going—seriously!

EASIEST COSMOPOLITAN

PREPARATION TIME: 2 minutes
SATISFACTION VALUE: Girls love it.
SERVES: 1

INGREDIENTS:

30ml (1 1/3 fl oz) vodka
15ml (2/3 fl oz) Cointreau
30ml (1 1/3 fl oz) cranberry juice
2 drops of lime cordial
20ml (1fl oz) fresh lemon juice

METHOD:

Pour all ingredients into a cocktail shaker. Shake, strain and serve into a nice looking glass.

I love Cosmos! They're so easy to make and to top it off, girls love them too. You can serve these with no ice, but I love to crush some ice and serve them.

CAPRIOSKA

PREPARATION TIME: 3 minutes
SATISFACTION VALUE: Loving life
SERVES: 1

INGREDIENTS:

1 lime, cut into wedges
30ml (1 1/3 fl oz) vodka
15ml (2/3 fl oz) sugar syrup or brown sugar
Ice
soda water

METHOD:

Squeeze lime wedges into the shaker, then chuck the skins in as well. Mash them up with the vodka and sugar syrup or brown sugar.

To crush the ice, place the ice inside a clean tea towel. Then take a rolling pin or a cricket bat and hit the tea towel. Transfer the ice to a tall glass. Pour cocktail mixture, including lime wedges, over the ice. Top with soda water.

MANGO DAIQUIRI

PREPARATION TIME: 3 minutes
SATISFACTION VALUE: Amazing
SERVES: 2

INGREDIENTS:

225g (7oz) frozen mango cheeks
60ml (2fl oz) white rum
60ml (2fl oz) mango syrup
1 teaspoon caster sugar
Ice

METHOD:

Blend and send, baby!

STRAWBERRY DAIQUIRI

PREPARATION TIME: 2 minutes
SATISFACTION VALUE: They will be lining up for more
SERVES: 2

INGREDIENTS:

225g (7oz) frozen strawberries
60ml (2fl oz) white run
60ml (2fl oz) strawberry liqueur
10ml (½fl oz) lime cordial
2 cups ice
30ml (1$\frac{1}{3}$fl oz) strawberry syrup

METHOD:

Whiz all ingredients together in a food processor! Serve garnished with a mint leaf if you want to be fancy.

One thing I have learnt from my restaurant, Tharen's, over the years, ladies love blended fruit cocktails.

BEERGARITA

PREPARATION TIME: 2 minutes
SATISFACTION VALUE: Funny as …
SERVES: 2 or 10, depending if you're drinking it as shots

INGREDIENTS:

30ml (1 1/3 fl oz) tequila
30ml (1 1/3 fl oz) Cointreau
30ml (1 1/3 fl oz) fresh lemon juice
10ml (½fl oz) water
10ml (½fl oz) sugar syrup
drop of honey
440ml (15fl oz) beer

METHOD:

Combine all ingredients—except beer—into a cocktail shaker and shake, baby, shake.

Pour into one glass or shot glasses—remember to leave some space at the top for the beer. Finish with a splash of cold beer in each glass—wicked.

A margarita with beer, you can either drink it as a cocktail or do it in shots at a party. Simple and so much fun.

PINA COLADA

PREPARATION TIME: 3 minutes
SATISFACTION VALUE: Totally tropical taste!
SERVES: 2

INGREDIENTS:

4–6 crushed ice cubes
60ml (2fl oz) white rum
30ml (1fl oz) dark rum
90ml ($3^{1}/_{3}$fl oz) coconut cream
Pineapple wedges, to decorate

METHOD:

Whizz the crushed ice in a blender with the white rum, dark rum, pineapple juice and coconut cream until smooth.

Pour, without straining, into a tall chilled glass and dress with pineapple wedges.

One of the younger generations of classics, this became popular during the cocktail revival of the 1980s and has reminded me of it ever since.

BLOODY MARY

PREPARATION TIME: 2 minutes
SATISFACTION VALUE: Bloody hell!
SERVES: 2

INGREDIENTS:

Dash Worcestershire sauce
dash Tabasco sauce
4–6 cracked ice cubes
60ml (2fl oz) vodka
15ml (2/3fl oz) splash dry sherry
180ml (5¾fl oz) tomato juice
juice of half a lemon
pinch of celery salt
pinch of cayenne pepper
celery sticks with leaves, to decorate
slice of lemon, to decorate.

METHOD:

In a cocktail shaker, pour the Worcestershire sauce and Tabasco sauce over ice and add the vodka, sherry, tomato juice and lemon juice.

Shake vigorously until frosty. Strain into a tall chilled glass, add a pinch of celery salt and a pinch of cayenne pepper. Then decorate with a celery stick and a slice of lemon.

This classic cocktail was invented in 1921 at the legendary Harry's Bar in Paris. There are numerous versions—some much hotter and spicier. Ingredients may include horseradish sauce in addition to, or instead of, Tabasco sauce.

BOBBY'S BIRTHDAY SPONGE

PREPARATION TIME: 30 minutes
COOKING TIME: 60 minutes
SATISFACTION VALUE: Happy Birthday!
SERVES: 4–6

INGREDIENTS:

100g (3½oz) butter
100g (3½oz) caster sugar
2 eggs, lightly beaten
1 teaspoon baking powder
100g (3½oz) flour
60g (2oz) strawberry jam
20g (2/3oz) icing sugar
100ml (3½oz) thickened cream

METHOD:

Preheat the oven to 190°C/375°F/gas mark 5. Get a stainless steel bowl and cream your butter and sugar together until white and fluffy. Add the egg and stir to combine.

Lightly sift in the baking powder and the flour into the butter mixture. Fold the dry ingredients through the mixture using a circular motion around the bowl. You can add a little bit of milk at this stage to adjust consistency if you like. The mixture should be able to drop off the spoon.

Grease your sponge tin or cake dish and pour your mixture in to it. Bake at 190 degrees for approximately 12–15 minutes.

Turn out on to a wire rack to cool. Take your time and cut the sponge in half using a bread knife. You need to be careful at this stage to make the halves even. Spread both sides with jam and whipped cream and place one on top of the other and dust with icing sugar.

WHIPPED CREAM OR CRÈME CHANTILLY:

Pour your thickened cream into a mixing bowl. Whisk and whisk, until soft peaks start to form. This is when the whisk starts to leave ribbons behind it when it moves.

Now mix in some castor sugar or icing sugar and whisk until thick. Turn the bowl above your head to see if it is done. IT SHOULD STAY IN THE BOWL AND NOT END UP ON YOUR HEAD!

Place candles on top and sing Happy Birthday!

Birthday cakes are often forgotten for birthdays. The wow factor of making your friend or girlfriend a cake for their birthday is amazing. Do this once and they will never forget it!

INDEX OF RECIPES

Babaganouj Dip	66
Baked Apples	98
Baked Potatoes with Cheesy Beans	26
Barbecue Garlic and Chilli Prawns	52
Barbecue Pork Chops	56
Beef Bourguignon with Wicked Mash	126
Beergarita	197
Best and Cleanest Scrambled Egg Fry-Up	162
Bloody Mary	206
Bobby's Bolognese	180
Bobby's Crème Brulee	141
Bobby's Birthday Sponge	204
Braised Lamb Shanks with Rice Pilaf	129
Braised Oxtail with Green Beans	125
Bread and Butter Pudding	120
Bresaola and Tomato Salad with Bocconcini	69
Caprioska	192
Champagne Cocktail	144
Cheese Platter	73
Chicken and Potato Soup	176
Chicken Kiev	28
Chocolate Thick Shake	168
Cola-marinated Lamb Chops	46
Creamy Potato Swirls	31
Crispy-Skin Ocean Trout with Cauliflower Puree	147
Easiest Cosmopolitan	191
Fish Finger Sandwich with Aioli	171
Grandma's 'bung in' Soup Poem	178
Grandma's Semolina with Blueberry Jam	89
Jug of Summer Pimms	55

Lamb Fillet Pastry with Parsnip Puree	114
Lemon Souffle	119
Lemon Tart	184
Marinated Barbecue Salmon	49
Mashed Banana and Ice cream	172
Mushroom Risotto	34
Mussels Without Thinking	134
Pan Fried Duck Breast with Caramelised Witlof and Buttered Potatoes	105
Pan Fried KingFish with Blanched Greens	84
Pea and Ham Soup	22
Pina Colada	198
Pork Shoulder with Baked Apples and Potatoes	96
Potato Wedges with Chilli and Garlic Aioli	152
Quiche Lorraine	74
Rhubarb and Apple Crumble	36
Roast Quail with Grapes and Cranberry Jus	108
Roast Rack of Lamb with Herb Crust	113
Sangria	188
Sausage Rolls	77
Sausage Sizzle with Beer, Onions and Tomato Relish	61
Schnitzel and Potato Rosti with Mushroom Sauce	165
Simple and Easy Lamb Cutlets	137
Spicy Vindaloo	155
Steak and Chunky Chips	40
Steak Tartar	83
Strawberry Daiquiri	195
Stuffed Shoulder of Lamb	24
Sweet and Easy Roasted Vegetables	101
Thai Green Curry	156
Traditional Tiramisu	62
Vanilla and Chocolate Panacotta	148
Whitlof and Rocket Salad	43
Whole Roast Chicken with Lemon and Thyme	95

First published in Australia in 2010 by
New Holland Publishers (Australia) Pty Ltd
Sydney • Auckland • London • Cape Town

1/66 Gibbes Street Chatswood NSW 2067 Australia
218 Lake Road Northcote Auckland New Zealand
86 Edgware Road London W2 2EA United Kingdom
80 McKenzie Street Cape Town 8001 South Africa

Copyright © 2010 New Holland Publishers (Australia) Pty Ltd
Copyright © 2010 © Text: Bobby Jewell for Chef Entertainment Pty Ltd
Copyright © 2010 Artwork/Design: New Holland Publishers Pty Ltd
Copyright © 2010 in photographs Chef Entertainment Pty Ltd, New Holland Publishers Pty Ltd and/or individual suppliers as credited.
Copyright © 2010 The Lad Chef: Chef Entertainment Pty Ltd as supplied under a non-exclusive licence to New Holland Publishers Pty Ltd

All rights reserved. No part of this publication may be reproduced,
stored in a retrieval system or transmitted, in any form or by any means, electronic, mechanical,
photocopying, recording or otherwise,
without the prior written permission of the publishers and copyright holders.

National Library of Australia Cataloguing-in-Publication entry

Jewell, Bobby.
The lad's chef/ Bobby Jewell.
1st ed.
9781742570129 (hbk.)
Includes index.
Cooking.
641.5

Publisher: Linda Williams
Publishing Manager: Lliane Clarke
Editor: Rochelle Fernandez
Designer: Emma Gough
Cover Photograph: Karen Watson
Food photography: Graeme Gilles/NHIL
Food stylist: Wendy Berecry
Karen Watson photography pages 4, 78, 32, 33, 81, 86, 122
(far left), 127, 139 (bottom), 159, 174 (far right), 182, 183, 203,
iStock images pages 78, 132 (2nd and 3rd), 139 (3rd)
Other incidental photography: Emma Gough/NHIL
Illustrations: Shira Livne
Production Manager: Olga Dementiev
Printer: Toppan Leefung Printing Limited

10 9 8 7 6 5 4 3 2 1